Luminos is the Open Access monograph publishing program from UC Press. Luminos provides a framework for preserving and reinvigorating monograph publishing for the future and increases the reach and visibility of important scholarly work. Titles published in the UC Press Luminos model are published with the same high standards for selection, peer review, production, and marketing as those in our traditional program. www.luminosoa.org

Leftover Women in China

*The publisher and the University of California Press Foundation
gratefully acknowledge the generous support of the
Sue Tsao Endowment Fund in Chinese Studies.*

Leftover Women in China

Understanding Legal Consciousness
through Intergenerational
Relationships

Qian Liu

UNIVERSITY OF CALIFORNIA PRESS

University of California Press
Oakland, California

Suggested citation: Liu, Q. *Leftover Women in China:
Understanding Legal Consciousness through Intergenera-
tional Relationships*. Oakland: University of California
Press, 2025. DOI: https://doi.org/10.1525/luminos.238

Cataloging-in-Publication Data is on file at the Library
of Congress.

ISBN 978-0-520-42307-7 (cloth)
ISBN 978-0-520-40574-5 (pbk.)
ISBN 978-0-520-40575-2 (ebook)

GPSR Authorized Representative: Easy Access System
Europe, Mustamäe tee 50, 10621 Tallinn, Estonia,
gpsr.requests@easproject.com

34   33   32   31   30   29   28   27   26   25
10   9   8   7   6   5   4   3   2   1

For leftover women

In memory of Shuzhen Wu (吴淑贞)

and Sue Hong Eng (伍叶瑞香)

CONTENTS

ACKNOWLEDGMENTS

Given the long process that research entails, this book would not have been possible without the support of my family, friends, colleagues, interviewees, and many other people who accompanied me during this journey; the Pacific Ocean and the Rocky Mountains, which always bring me peace and joy; and the backyard birds that constantly distract me from writing in order to teach me how to survive and even thrive in an increasingly challenging environment. This book is shaped, and in a sense, co-created by all these interactions and relationships.

I extend my gratitude to Maura Roessner, my editor at the University of California Press, who has enthusiastically supported this project from the outset, as well as Sam Warren and other staff members at the press who have been involved in the publication of this book. Thank you for taking on this project and for believing in its power. My thanks also to Sheila Berg for her excellent copyediting. I also must offer my thanks to three anonymous reviewers for their insightful feedback and trust in this book.

Over the decade during which this research was conducted, I had the privilege to have generous research participants and numerous colleagues who took the time to offer comments and help. I found my passion in legal consciousness and my identity as a law and society scholar at the 2016 Asian Law and Society Young Scholars' Workshop at the Faculty of Law, National University of Singapore. I am forever grateful to the organizers, mentors, and participants of the workshop for inspiring me and welcoming me to a community of like-minded scholars and friends. It was the love and support I received from that workshop that motivated me to frequent the Asian Law and Society Annual Meetings and the Law and Society Annual Meetings, where I met more scholars who became close colleagues and friends.

During my years at the University of Victoria, I was fortunate to be surrounded by mentors who not only provided insightful feedback but also lit up my journey with laughter and kindness, as well as colleagues and friends who were always generous with love, care, and words of encouragement. My colleagues at the University of Calgary have provided friendship, guidance, encouragement, and insight over the past three years. They have created an academic home for me to thrive and offered tremendous support for this project.

Fieldwork was carried out with the aid of a grant from the International Development Research Centre, Canada. The writing and rewriting of the manuscript benefited greatly from my ongoing conversations with members of the Chinese community in Alberta and British Columbia about family relations and social interactions in the past two years, which was made possible by the Social Sciences and Humanities Research Council Insight Development Grant. I am also thankful to the Department of Sociology and the Faculty of Arts at the University of Calgary, as well as the

University of California Press First Gen Program, for their support in making this book openly accessible electronically.

It is a difficult decision to not thank individuals by name in these acknowledgments, given my deepest gratitude to all of them. But I am reluctant to celebrate the completion of this book by listing some names and leaving out those who have contributed a great deal but cannot be acknowledged by name. I am grateful to my interviewees who trusted me with their stories. Their anonymous narratives are the heart of this book. Those who allowed me to interview them deserved to be named, but I am not willing to reveal their identities due to the sensitivity of this topic. I am also indebted to family members and friends who trusted me with their stories of abusive parents and family dramas, from which I learned to refrain from romanticizing intergenerational relationships. One of them has served as my sounding board, read through drafts word by word, and helped me identify concepts and assumptions that are not obvious to my Western audience. For privacy concerns, I hesitate to name any of them here. It was through hundreds of hours of conversations with them that I learned about the powerful impact our names can have on us. Our names constantly remind us of parental expectations and our connections with our families. For those who are lucky, names are good wishes and love from parents. For others, names are reminders of childhood traumas and ongoing connections with their abusers.

I must also share my deep appreciation for my parents, who encouraged my independent spirit and infinite curiosity from an early age. Like hundreds and thousands of Chinese parents, they always work hard to provide the best for me.

And thank you to my audience—for giving me the chance to share my feelings and findings with you. My story is embedded in the pages of this book, and perhaps yours is too.

Introduction

Sitting in a bubble tea house, Wei, a single woman in her late twenties and a civil servant in the city of Fuzhou, ordered a tofu dessert for herself and insisted on buying one for me. Wei is considered a "leftover" woman because of her "failure" to secure a marriage at this age. In China, if a woman is unmarried by the age of twenty-seven, people may see her as a leftover product in the market that no one is interested in purchasing. When we were discussing the pressure she felt to get married, Wei stopped, staring blankly at her dessert, and asked me whether I had heard of the Chinese proverb, "When a woman is in her twenties, she is like a flower in blossom; but if she is in her thirties, she is like soy pulp [女人二十一枝花，女人三十豆腐渣]." "Soy pulp" is the insoluble parts of soybean that cling to the cheesecloth left over from the process of making soy milk or tofu.

Before I figured out how to respond in a respectful way, Wei continued, "Many people I know still believe that only those women who 'have problems,' either physically or mentally, will remain single in their thirties and beyond." Wei was uninterested in romantic relationships and recognized that marriage would bring a double burden. She preferred to remain single, and eventually she would like to have children on her own or perhaps raise them with her close friend. But at the same time, Wei was worried that if she did not manage to enter a heterosexual marriage by the age of thirty, she and her parents would be buried in gossip and criticism. While she did not care about her nosy relatives, she felt extremely guilty about the pressure her parents had to face because of her leftover status. Wei confessed that if the pressure imposed on her parents became unbearable once she entered her thirties, she would probably surrender and get married to relieve her parents of this pressure.

Since she turned twenty-six, Wei had attended more than ten matchmaking events arranged by her relatives, but she never started a relationship. Her parents kept reminding her of the importance of attending these events out of their concern about the limited opportunities for working adults to meet potential marital partners. Wei's close relatives were actively connecting her with men they believed were a good fit as a way to help Wei's family "solve the problem." It was difficult for Wei to turn them down. "You must at least go to meet the guy to avoid consequences. I mean, if you don't pretend to put in the effort, those gossipy relatives will say that you are being too picky and no wonder you are left over in the marriage market," Wei explained.

Knowing that her parents were worried about her leftover status mainly because she might not be able to support herself and perhaps a child in the future, Wei planned to work hard so she would earn a promotion and salary increase. "With a successful career and financial independence," Wei said, "I am hoping to prove to my parents and other people that I can still have a decent life without a marriage and that I can have enough money to support a child on my own, in which case I think my parents won't be worried so much about me." Yet the law is standing in her way: childbearing outside marriage is prohibited under China's current legal framework, a reflection of China's commitment to the institution of heterosexual marriage. Her desire to get a promotion was part of her preparation for evading the law. If she could earn enough money, Wei would consider pursuing assisted reproductive technology services across the border, in the United States. At the same time, however, Wei knew little about how her plan would work out for her, as she had difficulty finding a role model who had gone down that path. Thus, Wei was not optimistic about her future. Throughout the interview, she emphasized several times that her resistance would probably falter.

Wei's struggle is not unique. There are approximately seven million so-called leftover women in China. The stigmatizing term "leftover women," which is pervasive in everyday conversations in China, refers to women in their late twenties and beyond who have never married. The derogatory label suggests that these women have failed to sell themselves in the marriage market at the best time and hence have become "leftover" products that depreciate rapidly. Chinese women arrive at their leftover status for different reasons: some prefer to remain single, some are not heterosexual, and others are still waiting for the right marital partner. These women struggle against parental expectations, social stigma, and legal constraints, all of which emphasize the importance of marriage and childbearing.

Parents often try hard to urge their daughters to get married during the "best" childbearing years. Some parents actively look for marital partners for their daughters by asking around, going to matchmaking events to meet parents of potential sons-in-law, or arranging matchmaking events for their daughters. Others push in a relatively subtle but still powerful way by displaying weakness and trying to instill guilt in their unmarried daughters, for example, by attributing their deteriorating health to the anxiety resulting from their daughters' leftover status. To make sense of their anxiety and efforts to push their beloved daughters into marriage, we need to understand the consequences of having a daughter who is considered left over in the marriage market. The stigma attached to such a daughter causes parents shame as relatives, neighbors, and colleagues consider it a failure of the whole family and keep asking the parents whether and when their daughters are going to get married. The Chinese state's promotion of marriage and stigmatization of unmarried women in the media in the past two decades further reinforce social stigmas.

Complicating this societal ostracization, under China's current legal system, women cannot have children outside marriage, nor do they have access to assisted reproductive technology services in China. The country's denial of same-sex marriage also means that nonheterosexual women have no hope of having children legally either on their own or with their same-sex partners. In other words, entering a heterosexual marriage is the only path for any woman to give birth legally in China. Given the law's denial of unmarried women's reproductive rights, parents of leftover women may end up having no one to continue the family line and visit their graves on the anniversary of their death. This is devastating for Chinese families, as descendants have the moral obligation to ensure the perpetuation of the family line so that ancestor worship continues in perpetuity.[1]

At the outset of this study, I was interested in how leftover women understood and dealt with the law's denial of their rights to become single mothers or choose same-sex marriage in mainland

China. Shortly after I started my fieldwork, I realized that leftover women cared more about the expectations and interests of their parents than what the law stipulated. Thus, I went on to ask: How are leftover women's strategies to deal with legal constraints shaped by intergenerational relationships and their filial obligation? What do their strategies tell us about ordinary citizens' relationships with the law? The more interviews and focus groups I had done to answer these questions, the more I realized that the broader community's expectations play a significant role in shaping leftover women's perceptions of parental expectations and thereby affecting the ways in which they relate to the law. This book demonstrates that leftover women tailor their strategies to deal with legal constraints according to their perceptions of their obligations within their families, communities, and society.

Leftover Women in China joins recent relational legal consciousness studies to reveal the process of co-constructing legal consciousness and the significant impacts of our close relationships on our legal consciousness. It associates itself with some of the most recent legal consciousness research that explores how people's thoughts and actions are shaped collectively with the thoughts and actions of those with whom they interact. "Legal consciousness" generally refers to the ways in which people experience, understand, and act in relation to law.[2] It is a concept that is much broader than legal awareness or legal knowledge, as people's decisions to turn to or against the law are both important subjects of legal consciousness scholarship.[3] In the law and society literature generally, relational studies of legal consciousness are an emerging framework for analysis. Building on critical analysis of Chinese family relations, research on gender and sexuality in China, multidisciplinary studies of leftover women, debates about "human quality" (*suzhi*), socio-legal studies of the relational self, and legal consciousness scholarship, this book aims to (1) facilitate a better understanding of the pattern of parent-child interactions that relies heavily on the sense of obligation and guilt; and (2) develop the concept of relation-based legal consciousness to capture how our sense of obligation resulting from relationships shapes our decisions to follow, evade, and even manipulate the law.

This book argues that our close relationships affect our legal consciousness not only through love and emotional intimacy but also through our sense of obligation and guilt. It is through a detailed analysis of the sense of obligation and the feeling of guilt resulting from leftover women's perceived failure to live up to their obligations as filial daughters that we can make sense of leftover women's strategies to deal with legal constraints. To facilitate a better understanding of leftover women's obligations and guilt, I now provide an overview of the political, legal, and social environment within which leftover women interact with their parents and relate to the law.

UNDERSTANDING LEFTOVER WOMEN'S OBLIGATIONS IN CHINA'S POLITICAL, LEGAL, AND SOCIAL CONTEXT

Despite the enormous pressure imposed on her by her parents, Wei was grateful for their support throughout the years. She had great sympathy for her parents and other parents of leftover women, seeing them as victims of China's strict implementation of the one-child policy and the lack of institutional support for the elderly. Wei planned her life, including her strategies to deal with the legal constraints of unmarried women's reproductive rights, according to what she believed to be her obligations as a filial daughter born and raised under the one-child policy.

The One-Child Policy and the Human Quality Discourse

Chinese families have been significantly reshaped by China's population policies in the past few decades. All the leftover women who participated in my research were born and raised under the one-child policy. It is impossible to understand leftover women's legal consciousness and their parents' concerns without discussing the role of these laws and policies in constructing family relations, shaping parental and societal expectations, enhancing marriage and childbearing as the only acceptable option, and imposing and sustaining inequality among leftover women with diverse backgrounds. Three decades of the implementation of the one-child policy have significantly changed family relations and the ways in which Chinese families function as a whole to deal with everyday tasks.

The one-child policy was first introduced in 1979 in China to curb population growth when the Chinese leadership was eager to develop the national economy after ending decades of political turmoil and international isolation.[4] At that time, China's large population was considered a barrier to economic growth. It led the leadership to introduce a nationwide one-child policy to control population growth and improve the "quality" of the population.[5] Under the one-child policy, with very few exceptions each couple in urban areas was allowed to have only one child, and in rural areas and among ethnic minorities a married couple could have a second child if the first one was female or disabled.[6]

In 2015, the universal two-child policy replaced the one-child policy, allowing all married Chinese couples to have two children. In May 2021, China announced the three-child policy, permitting couples to have up to three children to boost the birthrate. While the one-child policy is no longer effective, it has significantly shaped ordinary people's identities, social relationships, and Chinese family structures.[7] Scholars including Deborah Davis, Vanessa Fong, Harriet Evans, Esther Goh, Francine Deustch, and Peidong Sun have all touched on the influential role of the one-child policy in shaping Chinese family relations and the identities of both generations. Virtually all leftover women in my study mentioned that their identity as someone born and raised under the one-child policy led to feeling responsible to care for their parents and live up to parental expectations. Yunxiang Yan, an anthropology professor and Chinese family relations expert, considers the one-child policy a prime example of the statist nature of China's family laws and policy.[8] Yan introduces the concept of the "statist model of family policy making" to highlight the fact that the nation-state is entitled to control the economic and social lives of its people, as the interest of the state should be prioritized over that of citizens, individual families, and other communities.[9]

From the one-child policy to the current three-child policy, the law was never intended to grant unmarried individuals reproductive rights. Under China's population policies, only married couples are allowed to have children and access to assisted reproductive technology services, and at the time of my fieldwork the violation of the policy could lead to out-of-plan birth fines and other severe penalties.[10] Across China, medical professionals are prohibited from providing assisted reproductive technology services to unmarried individuals. An announcement posted on the State Council's website in April 2023 confirms that a marriage certificate must be presented for assisted reproductive technology services on social, ethical, and legal grounds.[11] Even if an unmarried woman managed to conceive using more accessible approaches such as at-home self-insemination with the sperm of known donors, she would still face barriers registering her child as a Chinese citizen and thus qualified for public education and healthcare.[12] In urban Xiamen in 2016, for example, an unmarried mother had to pay approximately 90,000 yuan (US$12,284) for her violation of the law before she could register her child.[13] Those who worked at public institutions could get fired for violating the family planning laws and policies.[14]

Because of these legal constraints, emergent feminist movements promoting single women's reproductive rights in China in the mid-2010s emphasized the connection between the law's denial of unmarried women's reproductive rights and the difficulties Chinese women faced to choose alternative family structures.[15] These feminist activists and LGBTQ lawyers put forward a joint report advocating legal changes to grant unmarried women the right to assisted reproductive technologies, as well as exemption from paying social maintenance fees, that is, the out-of-plan birth fine under China's population policy.[16] But legal constraints are only one piece of the puzzle when it comes to the one-child policy's impact on leftover women's choices of alternative family structures.

China's one-child policy has had a long-lasting impact on the ideal of families and motherhood, especially through the suzhi discourse. As a political keyword stemming from China's eugenics campaign during the promotion of the one-child policy, the term "suzhi" was officially designated to attribute China's failure to catch up with developed countries to the low quality of its population, especially in rural areas.[17] At that time, the Chinese government considered the country's population "too large, too rapidly growing, too rural, too ill-educated, and too uneven in age structure."[18] The solution, according to the Chinese state, was to produce and foster superior children who would grow into a high-quality labor force.[19]

To ensure the "quality" of the coming generations, the Chinese state put forward the eugenics campaign, which emphasized improvement of the genetic makeup, health, and education of children to meet the nation's needs.[20] The responsibility of nurturing high-quality children mainly fell on mothers: a good mother should sacrifice her own interests for her children and "follow the prescriptions of the latest science in conceiving, giving birth to, and rearing a high-quality child."[21] This emphasis on the mother's responsibility to ensure the quality of children has had a long-lasting impact on the criteria for qualified mothers in Chinese society.

At the same time, the suzhi discourse plays a role in justifying differential treatment among citizens with different backgrounds and resources. By the early 1990s, Chinese citizens' lack of suzhi had become "a general explanation for everything that held the Chinese nation back from achieving its rightful place in the world."[22] This is based on the assumption that the population in developed countries has higher suzhi than that of developing countries and that people who are considered to have higher suzhi will contribute more to the development of the country than those who are perceived to be of "low quality."[23] Since then, concerns about suzhi have pervaded everyday life and informed a wide spectrum of discourses and debates in Chinese society.[24]

In today's China, the suzhi discourse has become an indispensable part of social attitudes guiding people's behavior and their perceptions of others. In general, people use the term "high quality" to refer to elite and middle classness and to express their approval and respect for them. The term "low quality" is invoked to show disparagement or disapproval of others and describe so-called uncivilized behaviors.[25] The focus on the individual's suzhi shifts ordinary people's attention from the uneven distribution of resources and leads to the belief that people must compete with one another fiercely to accumulate suzhi in order to deserve more rights.[26]

Unsurprisingly, the suzhi discourse is effective in shaping leftover women's legal consciousness regarding the law's denial of unmarried individuals' reproductive rights. Influenced by this discourse, ordinary people in China, including parents and leftover women themselves, tend to divide unmarried women into "high-quality" women who deserve to have children on their own and "low-quality" women whose right to choose alternative family structures must be denied. As Wei's story demonstrates, leftover women generally believe that having a successful career and a good income is crucial if they want to raise a child on their own. Wei is in a much better place than most leftover women I interviewed in terms of financial status and educational background. Having a decent job as a civil servant and a bachelor's degree qualifies her as a so-called high-quality woman, preventing her from being accused of not understanding her own decisions if she decides to evade the law by turning to cross-border or underground reproductive care to become a single mother.

This emphasis on human quality has further reinforced existing inequality among leftover women of different backgrounds. On the one hand, it enables leftover women who have more resources in terms of education and money to believe that they have the right to ignore the law and choose alternative family structures. On the other hand, so-called low-quality women have the extra burden of justifying their decision to have children on their own. This book connects the human quality discourse with Michael Katz's theory of the undeserving poor to discuss how the emphasis on suzhi in Chinese society pushes some leftover women to comply with the law but leads others to evade or even manipulate the law.

The Phenomenon of Leftover Women

In the past few years, China has been promoting heterosexual marriage and childbearing, aiming to find a solution to its rapidly aging population resulting from the one-child policy. The current literature generally suggests that leftover women are suffering from enormous pressure to marry due to the state-media campaign that has stigmatized leftover women since the 2000s, as well as existing patriarchal cultures and gender norms in China.[27] In *Leftover Women: The Resurgence of Gender Inequality in China*, Leta Hong Fincher argues that the state-sponsored leftover women media campaign "serves as a state program to upgrade 'population quality' by pressing educated, 'high quality' women to marry and have a 'high quality' baby for the good of the nation."[28] Fincher further connects the Chinese state's promotion of marriage with its concern about the danger of having a large number of men who remain single involuntarily, as they could be "a threat to social stability."[29] Indeed, there has always been an assumption in Chinese society that men who fail to get married may turn to antisocial behavior and crime, linking them to the spread of violence, prostitution, sexually transmitted diseases, and the trafficking of women.[30] At the same time, Fincher suggests that the Chinese state uses the media to intimidate single women into marriage by promoting the idea that children born to women over thirty years old may have a higher risk of health problems.[31]

While the Chinese state's promotion of marriage has been one of the most important factors in pressuring leftover women to marry, it cannot work without the help of existing gender norms and patriarchal expectations in Chinese society. Sandy To, author of *China's Leftover Women: Late Marriage among Professional Women and Its Consequences*, accuses Chinese men of subscribing to a feudal, outdated, and patriarchal ideology and constraining leftover women's choices in marriage and childbearing.[32] She argues that the root cause of Chinese professional women's leftover status is patriarchal constraints in the marriage market: leftover women's professional and educational accomplishments are the greatest obstacle to marriage because their achievements have put too much pressure on their suitors, who are expected to have better careers and higher incomes than women.[33]

At the same time, the current literature on leftover women and media coverage of their dilemma tend to depict parents of leftover women as enemies and oppressors, accusing them of imposing patriarchal expectations on their daughters. To, for example, suggests that parents are constraining leftover women's marital choices because of their somewhat conservative, traditional, and backward beliefs, or what To calls "intergenerational differences in values."[34] According to To, parents, most of whom are traditional, continue to exert considerable control over their daughters' marital choices in China today.[35]

Leftover women are by no means merely victims of the state-sponsored media campaign and patriarchal culture, nor are they stereotypically stuck or desperate.[36] They contest gender norms by creating new identities and roles as independent women.[37] According to Yingchun Ji, a sociologist at Shanghai

University, leftover women are innovative actors who respond strategically to constraints and cultural disapprobation to construct a blend of modernity and tradition in their daily lives.[38] Many of them use their financial power to fight the stigma of being single and build legitimacy for an alternative lifestyle.[39]

Nevertheless, we should not assume that all leftover women are affected in the same way and to the same extent by China's laws and policies and its promotion of marriage. Despite the insightful discussions of the factors contributing to the phenomenon of leftover women, the existing literature's focus on autonomy and agency of heterosexual leftover women with successful careers marginalizes the voices of those who do not fall squarely within the category of high-quality and heterosexual women. Bringing the literature on the relational self and the discourse of suzhi into the picture and featuring the voices of leftover women from diverse backgrounds, this book offers a detailed analysis of how the law and social pressures disproportionately affect "high-quality" and "low-quality" women, as well as heterosexual and nonheterosexual women. More importantly, it calls for more attention to the role of parents in shaping leftover women's choices. It places leftover women's relationships with their parents and their sense of obligation as filial daughters and responsible citizens at the center of the discussion of their lived experiences and legal consciousness.

*Social Pressure and Anxious Parents
in the One-Child Nation*

The struggle of leftover women's parents has received little attention from scholars and the media. Aware of the struggles of my parents, I feel obligated to go beyond the assumption that they are merely traditional or conservative and instead situate their anxiety within the social, legal, and political environment. I cannot turn a blind eye to the support Chinese parents offer their children and the efforts they have made for their children's education and future, nor can I think of my parents as my enemies. My interest in leftover women's intergenerational relationships and legal consciousness came directly from my experience and the stories of many other leftover women around me when I was in my late twenties.

As the only child in my family, I used to be very close with my parents and grandparents and all my relatives. I called my parents every day and was happy to share with them every detail of my life and listen to their advice. Things changed when I reached my late twenties. I no longer enjoy my conversations with them as much when they take every opportunity to remind me of my status as a leftover woman. My grandmother lectures me every time I am on the phone with her, suggesting that I am supposed to bring a husband to show her as soon as possible. She keeps emphasizing that she is in her late eighties and cannot wait for long. I find myself reluctant to talk to her now, as the conversations are getting stressful. As a result, she blames my parents for not guiding me in the right direction. Many relatives and family friends share her opinion that my parents are responsible for my leftover status because it is their obligation to make sure that I have a happy family, namely, a husband and at least one child. Despite my educational and career achievements, my parents now feel a sense of shame among their relatives, friends, colleagues, and neighbors. Their friends and relatives always remind them that they should put more pressure on me to go down the "right" path.

To be fair, our relatives, friends, and neighbors are not necessarily making my parents uncomfortable out of bad intentions. They are aware of the cultural, political, and legal environment they live in, an environment that significantly disadvantages single women and their parents. After three decades of implementation of the one-child policy and the privatization of childcare and old-age support in China, it is a reality that the two generations must stick together to deal with everyday tasks for the best interest of the whole family.

The retirement age in China is among the lowest in the world as of 2024, letting women retire as early as fifty and men at sixty.[40] This allows grandparents time to devote to their multigenerational families.[41] Typically, the older generation who recently retired will provide childcare for their adult children who are busy with careers.[42] If their daughters forgo or delay marriage and childbearing, they cannot follow this timeline and plan their retirement life accordingly, which leads to a sense of uncertainty. Unsurprisingly, the importance of the so-called best childbearing age is among one of the most common reasons given by parents when they urge their daughters to marry before it is too late, an idea that has been reinforced in the media and everyday conversations.[43] After all, parents are aware that the only way to have children legally is in a heterosexual marriage. If their daughters keep delaying or even forgoing marriage, they may end up with no grandchild to carry on the family line. In addition, given the busy schedule of the younger generation and the lack of social support for the elderly in Chinese society, it is understandable for parents to want a son-in-law as additional old-age support.

RELATION-BASED LEGAL CONSCIOUSNESS

To make sense of leftover women's strategies to deal with legal constraints, this book presents the concept of relation-based legal consciousness, which captures both the impact of family relations on leftover women's legal consciousness and the process of the co-construction of legal consciousness in everyday life.

It builds on existing studies of relational legal consciousness to articulate how leftover women tailor their strategies to deal with legal constraints on alternative family structures according to their perceptions of parental expectations.

Relation-based legal consciousness shares the commitment to revealing the relational nature of legal consciousness with two other key concepts in existing law and society scholarship: relational legal consciousness and second-order legal consciousness. The notion of relational legal consciousness has been adopted by law and society scholars to refer to the relational approach to legal consciousness, the relational process of the formation of legal consciousness, and the legal consciousness resulting from this relational process.[44] Second-order legal consciousness, a concept introduced by Kathryne M. Young, focuses on the process of the co-construction of legal consciousness. It refers to "a person's beliefs about the legal consciousness of any individual besides herself, or of any group whether or not she is part of it."[45] Second-order legal consciousness, according to Young and Hannah Chimowitz, is a subset of relational legal consciousness. They suggest,

> We can think about relational legal consciousness as an umbrella term referring to any way that Person A's legal consciousness is shaped by their relationships to another person or group. This might include group membership, family dynamics, culturally constructed beliefs, and so on. In contrast, second-order legal consciousness can be understood as a more specific term that refers to how Person A's legal consciousness is shaped by Person A's perceptions of Person B's or Group B's legal consciousness—not simply by Person A's relationships to a person or a group generally. In other words, second-order legal consciousness refers to the processes via which Person A's legal consciousness is shaped by Person A's beliefs or impressions about the beliefs, attitudes, impressions, and inclinations of Person B (or any group) with regard to law.[46]

Relation-based legal consciousness represents another subset of relational legal consciousness that incorporates the important process captured by second-order legal consciousness but at the same time emphasizes the influential roles of relationships in shaping the individual's legal consciousness.

Current studies of the impact of relationships on legal consciousness have demonstrated that our close relationships tend to have a more powerful influence on our legal consciousness. In her discussion of how group identity interacts with law to motivate individuals to comply with the law, Janice Nadler suggests that often individuals are more concerned about what members of their in-group think than what most other people think, meaning that the most influential are those from the groups to which they have a strong desire to belong.[47]

Leisy J. Abrego argues in her article on the legal consciousness of US citizens in mixed-status families that "the narratives and experiences of loved ones are particularly meaningful—especially for those whose relatives are targeted by harsh laws and enforcement practices."[48] This relational nature of legal consciousness has been supported by my previous studies on how people in the same household and village help one another resist the one-child policy in rural China, as well as Hsiao-Tan Wang's studies on how Taiwanese family members make decisions regarding whether or not to invoke the language of law in family disputes.[49]

Relation-based legal consciousness draws on these studies and goes one step further by trying to capture the processes by which the individual's legal consciousness is shaped by these close relationships. To this end, I emphasize the need to define close relationships broadly to include closeness in terms of obligations. The sense of obligation is often a product of the individual's evaluation of the broader community's and the close ones' expectations regarding how an individual should behave: the individual constructs a version of obligation based on her interpretation of external information. The individual also participates in shaping these expectations in her everyday interactions with close ones and other members of her community.

As a subset of relational legal consciousness, relation-based legal consciousness acknowledges the highly relational nature of legal consciousness and at the same time focuses on the process during which the individual picks up cues and signals from daily interactions with family members and other people to construct her version of their expectations. This process involves being aware of social norms and expectations, reading between the lines, attending to both what has been said and what is left unsaid by close ones, and, more importantly, processing all the information through the lens of family interests to come up with what the individual believes to be the expectations of her close ones. The individual constantly refers to the broader community's expectations to evaluate what works best for her close ones and avoids bringing trouble to them.

Throughout this book, I use "broader community" to refer to unspecified people who participate in shaping the social norms and collective expectations in society and groups to which the leftover woman belongs. It is an abstract community. It has fluid and flexible boundaries, depending on who the leftover woman has in mind when she is trying to construct her version of parental expectations: it can be as narrow as people who live in the same neighborhood but can also be countless people from the past, present, and future in an abstract sense as long as the leftover woman believes that these people play a role in shaping and maintaining the moral standards of the larger society.

At the same time, a shared perception of the broader community's expectations is created through leftover women's interactions with specific people in their network of connections, such as relatives, neighbors, friends, and colleagues. The influential role of the broader community's expectations prompts me to use "relation-based" instead of "family-based" to describe leftover women's legal consciousness. As I show later, the broader community's expectations significantly affect leftover women's understanding of parental expectations and can sometimes trump what their parents have explicitly expressed.

Focusing on obligations enables a detailed analysis of the processes of the co-construction of legal consciousness. When it comes to leftover women and alternative family structures, it is crucial for these women to refer to the broader community's expectations of how a particular individual should relate to the law to be considered a responsible citizen; at the same time, in order to fit in and gain respect, individuals in Chinese society must demonstrate respect for the Chinese culture's emphasis on filial duty. Living up to the broader community's expectations in these two respects is essential; failing to do so entails consequences for their family's reputation and the interests of their parents. It is leftover women's strong desire to protect their parents and family interests that makes it extremely important to live up to the broader community's expectations. Thus, leftover women tailor their strategies to deal with legal constraints to ensure that their family relations and the reputations of their parents remain unharmed.

This book focuses on three strategies adopted by leftover women, namely, compliance with the law, evasion of the law, and manipulation of the law, all of which cannot be understood without foregrounding intergenerational relationships. For leftover women who decide to comply with the law and have children by entering a heterosexual marriage, the decision usually has little to do with their agreement with the law's denial of unmarried women's reproductive rights or their fear of legal consequences. It may merely be a by-product of their efforts to live up to the expectations of the broader community and parents.

Evasion of the law is closely related to and dependent on the legal consciousness of the broader community. As members of the broader community are generally willing to tolerate high-quality women's decision to have children on their own despite the law's denial of childbearing outside marriage, it reinforces leftover women's belief that their primary task is to accumulate resources and suzhi in order to be qualified to evade the law rather than advocate for unmarried women's right to have children. Their understandings of the law and how to evade it, therefore, are shaped by the broader community's legal consciousness.

"Legal evasion" in this book describes strategies adopted by leftover women to avoid all contact with the law or even resist it. As of this writing, legal evasion has attracted little attention from law and society scholars.[50] There is no clear definition of legal evasion. In general, law and society scholars consider evasion a form of small resistance, which is consistent with James Scott's definition of everyday forms of resistance.[51] Ignoring the law's imposition of license requirements and selling things on the streets is a typical example of legal evasion.[52] Building homes on land not officially designated for residential purposes or occupying public space illegally for personal use is another example. For leftover women, legal evasion includes turning to cross-border reproductive care and using underground and illegal reproductive services for the purpose of having children as a way to resist the law's denial of their rights to have access to assisted reproductive technology services legally in mainland China.

"Legal manipulation" describes the strategy of using the law to one's advantage by manipulating it for its imprimatur, which is typically appealing to nonheterosexual leftover women. Those who adopt the strategy of legal manipulation resist the law by entering into a heterosexual marriage with the purpose of getting out of it. Specifically, some nonheterosexual leftover women turn to "nominal marriage" (*xinghun*),[53] that is, a legal marriage between a gay man and a lesbian for the purpose of having children and pleasing their parents. Xinghun is essentially a performance to live up to one's filial obligation and the broader community's expectations. It is especially common among lesbian women who have decided not to confront their parents with their sexual identities.

Throughout this book, I discuss how parent-child interactions based on obligations and guilt lead to the lack of effective communication and thereby push leftover women to develop strategies to deal with the law's denial of alternative family structures.

ROAD MAP

The remaining chapters of this book build on one another to demonstrate how leftover women pick up cues from everyday interactions with their parents and constantly refer to the broader community's expectations to tailor their strategies to deal with legal restrictions. Chapter 1 discusses parents' anxiety that is caused by the social stigma attached to leftover women and how this anxiety prompts them to push their daughters into marriage. Three decades of strict implementation of the one-child policy in both rural and urban China has led to a high level of intergenerational interdependence among family members, as well as a strong sense of obligation among the younger generation to repay their parents' continuing support. Failing to live up to parental expectations and protect the family's reputation often gives rise to a feeling of guilt among leftover women. The chapter argues that the downflow of family resources, from the older generation to the young, in terms of housing and childcare provides the justification for parental intervention, while at the same time the sense of obligation and guilt among leftover women marginalizes their personal desires and jeopardizes effective communication between the two generations.

Motivated by the sense of obligation and guilt, leftover women are reluctant to confront their parents with their preference to remain single, have children outside marriage, or enter a same-sex partnership. This means that what leftover women describe as parental expectations are in fact constructed by these women rather than clearly articulated by their parents. This constructed perception of parental expectations then shapes leftover women's strategies to deal with legal restrictions. Chapter 2 introduces the concept of relation-based legal consciousness to understand the process whereby the broader community's expectations of the obligations of responsible citizens and filial daughters affect leftover women's legal consciousness through intergenerational relationships. It explains the reasons for the lack of interest in advocating for rights among ordinary citizens in relation-based societies and points to the importance of the broader community's expectations in figuring out parental expectations.

Chapters 3 and 4 focus on leftover women's resistance to the law through legal evasion and legal manipulation. When there is little hope of benefiting from challenging the law directly, leftover women develop strategies to either work around the law or use the law to their benefit. Chapter 3 analyses leftover women's desire to accumulate resources so that they are able to evade the law and obtain cross-border and underground reproductive care. It discusses how the political discourse of human quality, or suzhi, has significantly shaped leftover women's understandings of the law's denial of unmarried women's reproductive rights. It goes on to challenge the myth of suzhi by analyzing how so-called high-quality leftover women often end up with less ability to maneuver around the law's constraints because they are hemmed in by their prominent families' emphasis on reputation.

Chapter 4 discusses a subtler but powerful strategy adopted by nonheterosexual women to deal with the law's denial of same-sex marriage and unmarried women's reproductive rights. These women have either gone through or are considering the legal process of entering xinghun to live up to parental and societal expectations. It argues that the legal system's silence about homosexuality and the lack of both exit and voice options for leftover women lead to their manipulation of the law.[54] Stories of nonheterosexual women's use of the law to their advantage by entering xinghun enrich current studies of legal resistance and call for more attention to people's manipulation of the law for its imprimatur.

The concluding chapter summarizes the key contributions of this book and discusses the broader relevance of its findings for relational legal consciousness and parent-child interactions. By cultivating a relation-based approach to making sense of leftover women's strategies to engage with the law, I hope to provide sociolegal scholars with an innovative framework to study the relational nature of legal consciousness by bringing the co-construction of perceptions of the law into conversation with the impact of close relationships on our legal consciousness.

CHAPTER ONE

Anxious Parents and Filial Daughters in the One-Child Nation

On a humid Saturday morning, I went to the Magpie Bridge, a renowned matchmaking corner for parents located at the foot of Yu Mountain in Fuzhou. Such places exist in all major cities in China, attracting anxious parents who are eager to find a good match for their children. At around 8:30 a.m., parents from across Fuzhou started to gather. Hundreds of parents were busy reading basic information on young men and women, such as age, height, income, occupation, education, place of origin, and family background and assets, written on pieces of red and green paper clipped to string tied between trees. Parents walked around and exchanged information, trying to find a potential marital partner for their son or daughter.

"Hi, girl," a mother approached me, "you must be looking for a husband for yourself." Before I could respond, she tucked back my hair and started to examine my face. After I explained that I was a researcher conducting a study on leftover women, she immediately turned her back and walked away. I did not deserve her attention, as she preferred to spend her time on matchmaking.

Later, a few matchmakers tried to sell the contact information of male candidates to me, while others gave me business cards with information about their matchmaking services.

A few minutes later, Meng mama, a well-dressed woman in her early sixties, walked through the crowd to warn me of the danger of dealing with those matchmakers. Meng mama shared with me horrifying stories about how they took advantage of the enormous anxiety leftover women's parents were experiencing by selling them fake contact information or even hiring fake male candidates. "Some parents spent thousands of dollars only to find out it was nothing more than a scam," said Meng mama. According to her, approximately 80 percent of parents at the Magpie Bridge were looking for husbands for their daughters.[1] Meng mama was one of those parents until six months ago, when she managed to find her daughter a good match through her connections at the Magpie Bridge. Despite her success, Meng mama still came to the site every week to hang out with leftover women's parents and offer advice, hoping that her experience would be helpful to parents who were new to matchmaking.

What motivated Meng mama to come every week was her sympathy for anxious parents who had to work hard to "solve the most urgent problem of the whole family resulting from the one-child policy." Meng mama and her friends took it for granted that it was their obligation to help them with the dilemma. Meng mama emphasized, "It is the most basic responsibility of parents. We have to make sure the next generation has a partner and a child to take care of them when they are old." According to her, parents also had to take on the responsibility of caring for their grandchildren and provide housing for their adult children, both of which were impossible tasks without their help. In return, they expected their children to stay close, keep them company, and help out whenever necessary in their old age.

There are millions of parents in China who share this opinion with Meng mama. When their daughter is left over, they see it as a problem for the family to solve together. They believe that the entire family should work together to deal with challenges and tasks to ensure their survival and prosperity. Indeed, there are unbearable consequences for the entire family if the younger generation falls behind in marriage and childbearing. Parents of leftover women risk becoming targets of gossip and marginalization within their social networks. Having a daughter who is considered left over in the marriage market reflects badly on parents. As a result, parents become anxious and do whatever they can to find a good match for their daughters.

Not surprisingly, the vast majority of leftover women are against the idea of parental matchmaking and try their best to prevent their parents from "selling them in the marriage market like cheap goods."[2] When leftover women show their reluctance to participate in matchmaking events their parents have arranged, the parents complain about the younger generation's ingratitude. Meng mama believed that her daughter, Yun Meng, an editor at one of the leading media companies in the city, was too spoiled and naive to understand the unbearable consequences of delaying marriage and missing the best childbearing age. After fighting with Meng mama for three years, Yun finally surrendered and started dating a man Meng mama found for her. Despite her distaste for the man, Yun agreed to marry him just six months after they first met, which elated her mother.

In this chapter, I provide a detailed analysis of the tremendous pressure imposed on leftover women by their parents and explain why it is inescapable. The chapter discusses the pattern of parent-child interactions based on obligations and guilt in Chinese families. It starts with the reasons for the parents' pronounced anxiety concerning their daughters' leftover status and the importance leftover women place on meeting what they understand as their parents' expectations. It then illustrates the strategies adopted by parents to urge their daughters to get married. Drawing on narratives of leftover women and their parents, I demonstrate that effective intergenerational communication remains difficult in Chinese families. The moral duty of each family member to prioritize the interests of the entire family gives rise to a sense of guilt when the younger generation stresses individual desires and preferences that are likely to affect the family. This is especially the case when parents have done whatever they can to ensure that their daughters have a good education, housing, and childcare support. I challenge the conflation of the flow of resources from the older generation to the young and the lack of patriarchal power in Chinese families in the existing literature and call for a more nuanced understanding of Chinese intergenerational relationships. I argue that the intergenerational interdependence characterized by the downflow of family resources has marginalized the desires of leftover women within their families and jeopardized effective communication between the two generations about alternative family structures.

WHY DO PARENTS PUSH, AND WHY SHOULD LEFTOVER WOMEN CARE?

At a law and society conference a few years ago, I mentioned to a North American feminist legal scholar that leftover women worried more about parental expectations than legal constraints on their reproductive rights. She found it extremely difficult to understand why leftover women should care so much about parental expectations. She asked, "Why don't leftover women tell their parents to shut up and leave them alone? Why can't they ignore their parents and do whatever works best for themselves?" The idea of confronting parents or ignoring their expectations had never occurred to me, nor had it been mentioned by leftover women during my fieldwork. To feminist scholars who attach great value to autonomy, ignoring the pressure parents try to impose on them seems to be the solution for leftover women. However, parental expectations are inescapable in Chinese families when it comes to marriage, childbearing, and other personal choices that have the potential to affect the interests of the whole family.

To make sense of the extremely powerful influences of parental expectations on leftover women's legal consciousness, we need to understand why parents are so anxious when their daughters delay or forgo heterosexual marriage, as well as how Chinese family members depend on one another to deal with tasks and challenges in everyday life. The social stigma attached to leftover women has put enormous pressure on parents to urge their daughters to get married and have children. In addition, interdependence in multigenerational Chinese families resulting from the lack of affordable housing and childcare support in today's China further ties parents and their daughters closely together, making it extremely difficult for leftover women to ignore parental expectations.

Social Stigma Attached to Leftover Women
and the Impact on Parents

Remaining single carries a deep social stigma in China because marriage affords social and familial recognition that is otherwise unattainable.[3] People consider parents of leftover women "losers." If their daughter remains left over for a long time, people may accuse them of being irresponsible. This is because parents are supposed to be responsible for raising and guiding their children until they get married.[4] As Elisabeth Engebretsen suggests, in China, being single is widely seen as a personal failure that reflects badly on one's family and therefore comes at an emotional and material cost that is simply too high for most people.[5] Anyi, a feminist researcher who participated in my research to share both her own experience as a leftover woman and her understanding of gender relations in China, explained, "Having a daughter who is left over is similar to the scenario in which your friends' children all have offers from prestigious universities, but your daughter has not even been accepted to a community college." Central to Anyi's metaphor is the tendency of Chinese parents to compare the achievements of their children with others. It is a competition among friends, relatives, and colleagues, as the achievements of sons and daughters are generally considered successes of the parents. In fact, adult children's achievements serve as a source of self-esteem, respect, social status, and reputation for Chinese parents.[6]

Parents' conversations with friends and acquaintances about their daughter who is left over often induce anxiety, guilt, and self-doubt. Two years after my initial interview with Huang mama, she phoned me and complained about her experience at a reunion with classmates she had not seen for years. Huang mama had a successful career as a human resources manager in a state-owned company. Her daughter, Xuan Huang, had attended the best high school in town and a top university in China, after which she had gone to North America for graduate school and started her career there. Huang mama used to feel confident when seeing her old classmates given her daughter's academic achievement. Things suddenly changed when Xuan Huang reached her late twenties: Huang mama's friends and relatives started to ask about Xuan Huang's marital status.

At the reunion, Huang mama was criticized by the whole group shortly after her classmates found out that her daughter was still single. "My classmates accused me of not being a responsible mother. They told me that it was a big mistake for me to let my daughter go overseas. Some guys even told me to ask my daughter to come back immediately to get married in order to relieve our stress," said Huang mama. She described the party as a "denunciation meeting [批斗会]," a term that was used during the Cultural Revolution in China to refer to public gatherings held for the purpose of criticizing, denouncing, and mocking people in front of thousands. Others at the reunion reminded Huang mama of the risk of having no grandchild if she failed to take action to urge her only child to give birth during the best childbearing age. "You are going to miss the joy of grandparenting. And no one will carry on your family line and visit your grave in a few decades from now," Huang mama's classmate warned her. Huang mama felt that her whole family was under attack because of her daughter's leftover status. The experience was so painful that Huang mama decided that she would not attend another class reunion until her daughter got married.

Sun mama, mother of a thirty-four-year-old woman, had a similar experience. Sun mama used to participate in Chinese square dancing in her neighborhood with a group of middle-aged and retired women after dinner almost every day. They danced to songs played on a brick-sized portable music player in a park and would chat during the break. Sun mama decided to quit after constantly being asked about her daughter's marital status. Surrounded by those who were always bragging about their lovely grandchildren and their daughters' happy marriages, Sun mama felt a strong sense of shame whenever those women asked whether and when her daughter was going to get married. Uncomfortable conversations about a daughter's leftover status can happen anywhere with anyone—at the dinner table with relatives and friends, in an elevator or hallway with colleagues or neighbors, and even in grocery stores when bumping into acquaintances.

I can imagine the North American feminist legal scholar asking me why Huang mama and Sun mama had to care so much about what other people thought about their daughter's marriage. Why not just ignore them or ask them to change the subject? To answer this question, it is necessary to discuss the importance of "face" in front of members of their family and community. "Face" can be loosely defined as the recognition by others of an individual's social standing and moral reputation.[7] It is what a person feels about her image as seen through the eyes of others.[8] No one will deny the significance of having face to an individual's dignity and the unbearable consequences of losing face in Chinese society. Fei Wu, author of *Suicide and Justice*, notes, "Face is important not only because it is a symbol of personhood, but also because it is the essence of human dignity."[9] As I have argued elsewhere, dignity is a relational concept in China; it is highly dependent on other people's attitudes.[10] People who are immersed in collective cultures tend to rely on other people's assessments of whether they have fulfilled social obligations so as to gain and maintain dignity.[11]

If a person is looked down on in the community, she cannot possibly maintain good *guanxi* with others.[12] Guanxi, loosely translated as networks of social connections or ties,[13] is linked internally to face. Yanjie Bian, author of *Guanxi: How China Works*, defines the term as "a dyadic, particular, and sentimental tie that has the potential for facilitating the exchange of favors between the two parties connected by the tie."[14] Ordinary people's desires to maintain good guanxi make having face crucial in their everyday lives: severe loss of face places the individual and their family in a despised and isolated position, which reduces the opportunities for both the individual and their families to use social networks to obtain resources.[15] As Lawrence Hsin Yang and Arthur Kleinman suggest, the cultivation and maintenance of face are key to allowing individuals membership in guanxi networks in China, which determines the resources these individuals can mobilize within these networks.[16] The importance of having face in maintaining guanxi pressures individuals to do whatever they can to avoid losing social recognition and endangering established guanxi networks. Thus, people must constantly adjust their behavior and thoughts according to dominant social norms in order to fit in with the rest of the group, whether dancers or former classmates.

At the same time, as I discussed in the introduction, friends and relatives do not necessarily comment on parents' unmarried daughter out of bad intentions. Some may genuinely be concerned that the parents could lose face and social connections because of their daughter's failure to get married. Leftover women's parents are supposed to respect people's "good intentions." Even if the parents suspect that others might be simply using their daughter's leftover status to tease or shame them, the importance of face and guanxi pressures them to always appear to be grateful for "good intentions."

The social stigma attached to leftover women has a significant impact on the everyday lives of their parents. As we learned from the stories of Huang mama and Sun mama, their daughters' leftover status took away their confidence and face in front of other people, as social gatherings can be easily turned into "denunciation meetings." The sense of losing face forces these parents to give up social activities they used to enjoy and isolate themselves in order to avoid unpleasant conversations about their daughters' leftover status.

Seeing their parents suffer from social pressures, some leftover women decided to change their timeline and criteria. Sun mama's daughter, Hangyan Sun, felt obliged to settle down shortly after Sun mama quit the square dance group. She made the decision to marry her current husband in just one month, even though she felt he was not good enough for her. While Hangyan did not care about what the dance group members said, she was concerned about her mother's mental well-being and wanted to ease her worries. It was Hangyan who told me about Sun mama's experience. She used the story to explain why she felt so guilty about causing her mother stress, considering the years of care, love, and support she received from her. After getting married, Hangyan's husband moved in, and the two generations lived together in her parents' house. This arrangement has become increasingly more common in China as most adult children have to rely on their parents for housing and childcare.

The Downflow of Resources in Chinese Families

Three decades of the implementation of the one-child policy challenged the traditional notion, "the more children, the better [多子多福]," and made small families the norm for most Chinese people. In these small families, the only child often receives all the love and attention of parents and even grandparents.[17] Most family resources tend to flow downward to the child, and the focus of the whole family shifts from worshipping the ancestors to caring for the younger generation.[18] Many low-income parents sacrifice their own needs by skimping on necessities or working long hours to support their children.[19] Even after the younger generation grows up and has its own nuclear families, Chinese parents continue to feel responsible to help their adult children with housing and childcare.[20] As of my fieldwork in the late 2010s, most leftover women I interviewed were still financially dependent on their parents.

The extreme unaffordability of housing in urban China makes it almost impossible for the younger generation to purchase a home without the help of parents. Parental financial help was common among young home owners across China.[21] At the same time, as inflexible work schedules and overtime have been the norms in China, grandparenting is crucial to the career development of the younger generation.[22] For most Chinese families, the only way to survive is to work as a team to gather resources to buy homes for the young couple and care for their offspring.

Guan mama, a delivery driver for a state-owned factory, bought a two-bedroom condo for her daughter in a new community on the edge of the city of Xiamen in 2015. Guan mama and her husband, a salesman in the food industry, saved every penny and sold their old home to buy the place for their only daughter. They wanted to make sure that she would at least have a home if she had difficulty finding a husband who could provide housing. Guan mama complained, "A condo in Xiamen usually costs around 5 million yuan (approximately US$690,000). It is impossible for the younger generation to buy one without parental support. Our generation must help our singles purchase homes because we don't want our only child to suffer." Guan mama's daughter worked as a court clerk in urban Xiamen, which was considered a decent job. However, with her monthly income of approximately 7,000 yuan (approximately US$970), buying a home would be unthinkable without parental support. Guan mama did not blame her daughter; she understood that the housing crisis in China was too big a social problem for her daughter to handle on her own.

Lufang, a thirty-year-old bank clerk, was one of many leftover women who laughed when I asked whether they were supporting their parents financially. Lufang said, "Nowadays, parents don't expect financial support from us, nor do we have the capacity to support them. My income can barely cover my own living expenses in a city like Xiamen. It is me who always ask them for help." Lufang had never thought of being able to afford a condo in Xiamen, let alone buy one for her parents. She had been evicted from rentals seven times within two years since she moved to the city in 2014. It was a period when the housing market was strong, and owners seized the opportunity to sell their properties.

Seeing Lufang move from place to place, her father decided to borrow from the bank to speculate on the stock market in order to give her a down payment. They got lucky, and Lufang happily bought a small condo near her workplace. Looking back, Lufang realized how risky it was for her father to have such a crazy plan that could easily ruin his retirement. However, that was not the first time her family took a risk for her. Lufang recalled that in the early 1990s, her parents spent all their savings so she could attend the best elementary school in town. She was grateful that her parents did whatever they could to support her without asking anything in return. She felt it would be inappropriate to ignore their expectations considering the support she had received from them.

Recent studies find that many parents subsidize their children's purchase of a home and renovations in order to strengthen the sense of intimacy with their children: some parents provide the down payment; others pay in full.[23] These parents, as Xiaohui

Zhong and Shining He suggest, support their children's purchase of a home in the hope of "communicative intimacy" with their children.[24] This type of intimacy emphasizes constant communication and involvement in one another's everyday lives and continuing exchange of material and financial support whenever needed.[25] According to Suowei Xiao, "By willingly providing financial resources, parents capture the chance to take part in their children's family affairs and to cultivate a relationship characterized by emotional exchange, respect, and close ties."[26] The downflow of resources in terms of housing support, therefore, motivates many adult children like Lufang to repay their parents. As Jieyu Liu argues, "The increase of both emotional affection and the material interest reinforce, rather than weaken, children's filial obligation towards their parents."[27]

In addition to housing support, providing childcare is another common strategy used by parents to nurture a sense of filial obligation in their adult children and maintain emotional bonds with them.[28] Indeed, most leftover women expect their parents to provide childcare in the future due to their busy schedules and the lack of reliable and affordable childcare services, since daycare is a for-profit industry in China. Almost all leftover women I interviewed agreed that it would be impossible for them to keep their jobs without relying on grandparenting. Complaints about the incompatibility of work and childcare in China came up frequently in my interviews with leftover women. In fact, grandparenting is an increasingly common practice in both rural and urban China; it is widely considered a key adaptive strategy to maximize the well-being of the extended family.[29]

Grandparenting used to be provided primarily by the husband's parents due to China's long history of patrilineality. Maternal grandparents are commonly referred to as "outside grandmother" and "outside grandfather," indicating that maternal grandparents are more distant from their grandchildren than are paternal grandparents.[30] However, the one-child policy has made the 4-2-1 pattern one of the most common family structures in China: a married couple who are both only children have one child and four parents (including parents-in-law).[31] "Outside grandparents" without sons, therefore, can devote their time to their daughter's child. As the wife is expected to be the primary caregiver for the child, many outside grandparents consider grandparenting a way to help reduce the burden of their daughter who is occupied with work.

Almost every mother I interviewed mentioned concern about the difficulties of their daughters' living with the mother-in-law; therefore, they were willing to help with childcare if their health allowed.[32] When I was conducting a focus group with mothers of leftover women in Aunty Hong's teahouse, Aunty Hong, who was making tea for us, casually warned the group of the danger of relying on mothers-in-law for childcare: "My daughter disagreed with her mother-in-law about how to take care of the little one. The overbearing mother-in-law kept accusing my daughter of being ungrateful in front of the whole family. In the end, my daughter chose to divorce." Mothers who participated in the focus group were all willing to shoulder the responsibility of childcare for the best interests of the whole family. This also contributes to the anxiety among leftover women's parents, as they are genuinely worried that their deteriorating health may not allow them to care for their grandchildren if their daughters delay childbearing.

In summary, social stigma leads to tremendous pressure on the whole family to work together to get rid of the daughter's leftover status. The housing crisis and the need for grandparenting further reinforce intergenerational interdependence. When the whole family is under attack, family members feel obliged to work together and prioritize family interests over individual desires.

Thus, the boundary between individual desires and familial needs becomes blurry and fluid. As I discuss in the next section, parents actively ask their daughter to get married as soon as possible; and the failure to prioritize family interests often leads to a profound sense of guilt among leftover women.

PARENT-CHILD INTERACTIONS BASED ON THE SENSE OF GUILT

Given that parents are willing to sacrifice their own interests for a better life and the future stability of the younger generation, adult children often feel compelled to surrender their personal desires to family interests. I heard one leftover woman after another express their strong desire to repay their parents' support, as well as a profound sense of guilt for failing to fulfill their filial obligations. I propose that the downflow of family resources and the younger generation's dependence on grandparenting have further marginalized the personal desires of leftover women. When the idea of prioritizing the whole family's interests dominates their conversations, it jeopardizes effective communication between parents and daughters and can sometimes transform into moral blackmail. The difficulties of having effective conversations push some leftover women to consider evading or manipulating the law to live up to parental expectations.

Strategies to Instill Guilt and Urge Filial Daughters to Get Married

I identified two common strategies adopted by leftover women's parents, which I refer to as "pushing bluntly" and "displaying weakness." Both strategies put pressure on leftover women to enter a heterosexual marriage for the interest of the family.

1. Pushing bluntly. Parents who adopt the strategy of pushing bluntly actively participate in matchmaking or explicitly remind their daughter of her filial duty to get married and have children. To some extent, participating in parental matchmaking is a way for some parents to express their love, care, and support, as most of them are genuinely worried about their daughter's future. As Jun Zhang and Peidong Sun suggest in their research on parental matchmaking, parents who are active at the matchmaking corners are driven by their sense of duty and responsibility to help their children find a suitable spouse.[33]

Their aggressive and confrontational approach, however, inevitably jeopardizes family relations and reduces the chance of effective communication between the two generations. When parents have no luck at the matchmaking corner, they tend to take out their frustrations on their daughters. When I met with Meng mama's daughter, Yun Meng, she complained about Meng mama's aggressive matchmaking in the past three years. She said,

> You have no idea how much pressure my mum had caused. We quarreled a lot. Before I found my partner, I did not have any space to take a break from all her craziness. She forced me to spend all my time on matchmaking and asked me to reduce the time spent on "irrelevant" things such as hanging out with friends and playing piano. She was very stubborn and refused to listen to me. Now I have found a partner, and she is finally happy. And I am relieved—I have gained more than ten pounds in the past few months.

Unfortunately, given the large number of anxious parents at the marriage corners across China, Yun's experience is not unique. Confronted with extreme aggressiveness, many leftover women find it impossible to reason with their parents.

Some parents even equate the younger generation's delay of marriage with being unfilial. Guan mama, the mother who bought a condo for her daughter, was one of them. She described women who remained single at the age of thirty as "selfish and self-centered daughters who don't mind hurting the feelings of their parents." My status as an unmarried woman did not discourage Guan mama from openly expressing her disdain for leftover women. Later in the interview, she even started lecturing me by emphasizing the need to fulfill my filial obligation instead of focusing on my own life. It turned out that the very fact that I left my parents to go overseas did not sit well with her either. Guan mama urged me to be filial by putting myself in my parents' shoes and staying closer to them.

While I appreciated that she might have good intentions, I could not help but wonder whether Guan mama's criticism of the younger generation's delay of marriage had affected her daughter's decision. If Guan mama kept lecturing her daughter this way, her aggressive approach would have much in common with Meng mama's strategy and should count as pushing bluntly, even though Guan mama had never gone so far as to participate in parental matchmaking. Guan mama's belief reflects a prevalent misunderstanding of leftover women's intentions in Chinese society. In fact, most leftover women care about their parents and are trying their best to fulfill filial obligations. The more filial they are, the more stressed they feel when they remain single.

In a Starbucks near the Xiamen railway station, I met with Shanna, a twenty-seven-year-old single woman with large eyes and tanned skin. Shanna's mother was among the most active participants at parental matchmaking events across the city and was a typical parent who pushed bluntly. Shanna's mother spent at least two days a week attending these events, even during heat waves and on cold winter days. She often came home feeling disappointed and started scolding Shanna for being unfilial and selfish. Throughout the interview, Shanna told me repeatedly that she was on the brink of a mental breakdown because her mother had put so much pressure on her to find a partner.

Shanna was far from unfilial, irresponsible, or emotionally immature. She took every opportunity to express her love for her mother. However, all her efforts turned out to be futile because her mother was so preoccupied with finding a good match for her. Shanna said:

> I have suggested many times that we should spend the weekend doing something fun together, such as going hiking and visiting a local park. I also offered to take my mother out for dinner. However, she always refuses by saying that her primary task is to go to the matchmaking corners to find me a husband. Whenever I suggest that she should at least take a break, she always says that she does not want to miss any opportunity.

Shanna felt guilty that she was not able to save her mother the trouble of spending all her free time at matchmaking corners. She tried to make up for it by volunteering to do all the housework. However, her mother never seemed to be satisfied. In the months prior to the interview, Shanna found herself spending more and more time in the gym, consciously or unconsciously avoiding going home to be under the same roof with her mother. Going to the gym was one of the few activities her mother approved of, as girls with good figures were considered more desirable in the marriage market.

To deal with her mother's blunt pushing, Shanna had developed a series of tactics to resist: she agreed to attend the matchmaking events her mother arranged but tried to keep a "resting bitch face" all the time; she told her mother that she was busy attending matchmaking events when she was actually hanging out with friends; she ignored the messages from people she met via matchmaking and told her mother that those guys thought she was not good-looking enough to be their wife. Through these tactics, Shanna could occasionally take a break.

When parents push bluntly, they are unintentionally but inevitably pushing their beloved daughters away. This aggressive approach leaves little room for effective communication between the two generations. Some anxious parents, such as Meng mama and Shanna's mother, translate their daughter's lack of interest in matchmaking into her reluctance to fulfill her filial obligations and prioritize family interests. It is as if her other achievements and contributions to the family do not matter at all. Under these circumstances, parents may even interpret their daughter's efforts to express her own desires as confronting them with her selfishness.

2. Displaying weakness Not all parents are as persistent and aggressive as Meng mama and Shanna's mother or as candid as Guan mama. Most parents adopt strategies that seem subtle to convey their expectations and pressure their daughters, which I refer to as displaying weakness. They often emphasize their deteriorating health and attribute it to their daughter's marital status. Within this category, there are various types of strategies.

The most common strategy parents adopt is to express their eagerness to help their daughters with childcare and emphasize that they will not be able to offer as much support when they get older. Gao mama and Gao baba had both retired a few months before my interview with their daughter, Jiani Gao, a single woman in her late twenties who was enthusiastic about furthering her career as a barista. Gao mama and Gao baba asked Jiani to give them a grandchild to keep them busy. Jiani did not see anything wrong with being frequently reminded of the need to have children: "They are just getting bored after retirement and want to contribute something to our family. They hope I give birth when they are still energetic so that they can help with childcare and leave me more time to focus on my career development." Indeed, as Esther Goh's research on childcare under the one-child policy in Xiamen documents, many retirees believe that caring for grandchildren is the best thing they can do after retirement.[34]

Some parents focus instead on the possibility that grandchildren will bring them energy, optimism, youthfulness, and a sense of purpose. Linying, a single woman in her early thirties, felt responsible for her father's depression in recent years. Her father enjoyed spending time with young children and wanted a grandchild badly. He kept reminding Linying that he would feel much happier and healthier if she gave him a grandchild, citing recent studies to suggest that intimacy with grandchildren could reduce depression and lead to the grandparent's greater longevity. "Sometimes I feel bad seeing him depressed and think I am responsible for his poor health. At times, I feel I should probably rush into marriage and have a child just for my father," Linying said. She continued, "When they are so worried about my marital status, nothing can make them happier than seeing me get married and have a kid."

Along the same lines, some parents attribute their insomnia, high blood pressure, and gray hair to their anxiety about their daughter's leftover status, with the intent to guilt them into marriage. By displaying weakness, these parents use their daughters' filial piety and genuine love for them to urge their daughters to get married and have children. It is, according to some leftover women, "moral blackmail in the name of love."[35]

It may seem that displaying weakness is a better strategy than pushing bluntly. A nonconfrontational approach, however, does not necessarily mean less pressure on leftover women, especially those who are eager to appease their parents. For leftover women like Linying, although her father had never gone so far as to attend parental matchmaking events, she felt the pressure getting stronger every minute. On the surface, leftover women who are urged in this way enjoy relatively harmonious family relationships with their parents; however, the guilt of not being able to meet their parents' expectations when they are in poor health haunts filial daughters, making it almost impossible to take a break from the pressure. Displaying weakness affects filial daughters much more than those who are "selfish" enough to confront their parents and resist the pressure directly.

The strategies of pushing bluntly and displaying weakness both give rise to a sense of guilt among the younger generation. The former focuses on blaming leftover women for not fulfilling their filial obligations and trying to guilt-trip them into marriage; the latter attributes the parents' illness at least partly to anxiety resulting from their daughter's leftover status. It is worth mentioning that parents who push bluntly, such as Meng mama and Shanna's mother, are trying their best to fulfill their own obligations as parents to help their daughters "solve the problem." It is their hard work and support, more than the behavior of accusing their daughters of being immature and selfish, that contributes to the sense of guilt among leftover women. These strategies pressure the younger generation to get married and have children as soon as possible for the interests of the family. The pressure on individuals to make sacrifices for the family, however, prevents them from genuinely understanding each other's needs.

It leads to a profound sense of guilt that increases leftover women's anxiety and pushes them to rethink their choices in marriage and childbearing.

The Power of Guilt and Filial Daughters' Pressure

There was a shy smile on Wei's face when she said she really believed that her parents should control her life. Wei, whose story was introduced earlier, confessed:

> If I end up getting married, I am doing it for the happiness of my parents. That's why their opinions are so important to me—I would be doing it for them. I don't think I am ready for a romantic relationship—to be honest with you, I cannot imagine being together with a man. It is too scary. But I am willing to get married to meet the expectations of my parents and ease their anxiety because I am grateful for all their support. I am happy to let them control my life as a way to return the favor.

Wei asked whether I thought she was brainwashed by so-called traditional Chinese culture into unconditional obedience to her parents. "After all, they sacrificed a lot for me," Wei said before I had a chance to respond.

Wei's insistence on living up to her parents' expectations because of the sacrifice they made is a recurring theme in my interviews with leftover women. As Liu notes, despite the decline in everyday financial and instrumental support by adult children for their parents, intergenerational interdependence has become stronger for the one-child generation because of their greater dependency on their parents.[36] In fact, the feeling of guilt is not an entirely new concept in studies on intergenerational relationships in China. Vanessa Fong, author of *Only Hope*, describes the power of guilt as the younger generation's emphasis on repaying the sacrifice made by their parents and the hardship parents endured to ensure a better future for the children.[37] According to Fong, the idea that parents were suffering in terms of material constraints and even illness so that their children would have a better life "induced guilt and a heightened sense of filial obligation in their children."[38] Harriet Evans's 2008 research on mother-daughter relationships in China reveals that daughters' awareness of their parents' efforts reinforced their desire to "give something back" to them, which often means the need to show their gratitude by living up to their mothers' desires that they marry appropriately and have children.[39]

Building on the findings of Fong and Evans, my analysis of leftover women's sense of guilt goes one step further by explicitly linking "guilt" with "obligations" to distinguish the former from reciprocal love. While the differences between the two seem subtle and some leftover women may even use the two interchangeably to describe their motivations to live up to parental expectations during the interviews, guilt differs from reciprocal love in that the former is closely associated with the broader community's expectations of filial daughters and these daughters' failure to fulfill their obligations. I argue that unlike reciprocal love, which promotes intimate communication between the two generations, guilt takes up, even perhaps eliminates, the space for equal and effective communication between the two generations. In other words, interdependence among leftover women and their parents and the downflow of family resources are by no means evidence of "inverted generational hierarchy" or "post-patriarchal intergenerationality."[40] When it comes to marriage and childbearing, the sacrifices and hard work of parents become the justification for parental intervention and authority.

I have no intention of discounting the love and care parents have for their daughters. I remain deeply grateful for all the support my parents gave me and have a great deal of respect for parents who support their children's education, housing, and childcare, among many other things. When I asked those parents what they expected in return for their sacrifice for their children, none of them believed they could rely on the younger generation for financial support and elderly care. Instead, parents frequently brought up the notion of self-reliance. Guan mama said, "I think parents cannot ask for too much from the only child. We will be satisfied as long as our child thinks of us often and comes to visit us when they have time. Honestly, our generation, in general, does not expect any financial support from the younger generation. . . . They do not have the money and resources to support us." Guan mama's opinion is one that is common in both urban and rural China. As Yu Xie and Haiyan Zhu's quantitative study on intergenerational financial support in urban China demonstrates, a large number of adult children receive financial support from their parents rather than the other way around. Xie and Zhu argue that monetary support to aging parents in urban China is rather symbolic: elderly parents consider those "symbolic transfers" their adult children's expression of love, with many of them eventually transferring the money back to their children.[41] Similarly, according to another study focusing on urban China, "the majority of families are engaged in an exchange relationship, in which parents typically offer material support in return for care and/or emotional support."[42] Even in rural China, where seniors are not able to offer as much financial support as their urban counterparts, many people of Guan mama's generation are working hard to save extra money, participating in the rural pension system, and purchasing commercial insurance for retirement.[43]

Yunxiang Yan, a leading scholar in the area of Chinese family and kinship, introduces the concept of the inverted family to suggest that the power relationship in Chinese families has been turned upside down since the strict implementation of the one-child policy. According to Yan, "The most widely recognized indicator of the inverted generational hierarchy is the constant decline of parental authority and power and the parallel increase in youth autonomy and freedom in both urban and rural Chinese families."[44] Yan further suggests that the generations born in the 1980s and after are often clueless about patriarchal power in intergenerational relations, as "they have grown up with tremendous space and freedom to negotiate with their parents and grandparents every aspect of family life."[45] While some recent studies on Chinese family relations support Yan's findings,[46] the conflation of the two ideas, namely, the downflow of resources and the lack of patriarchal power in Chinese intergenerational relations, does not seem to reflect leftover women's experiences.

If leftover women truly had space and freedom to negotiate with their parents for everything, they could simply inform their parents that they are not interested in or at least not ready for a heterosexual marriage. There would be no need for them to gain approval from their parents to remain single or choose alternative family structures. Unfortunately, Wei, Lufang, Hangyan, and many other leftover women are not free of the burden of guilt: when the older generation gives whatever they have in order to provide housing and childcare, meeting parental expectations and fulfilling filial obligations inevitably become a burden adult children have to bear.

After realizing how much anxiety and pressure her parents felt, Lufang decided to marry a man she had turned down a long time ago, a man she believed was immature, spoiled, and self-centered. Lufang confessed that she had not married for herself but out of her obligation to protect her parents from people who were talking absolute nonsense about her leftover status. Lufang said, "I don't think marriage is a must. I only got married to free my parents from the pressure imposed on them by those gossipy and nosy relatives, as well as to ease all their worries about my future. After all, my parents have sacrificed so much and are always ready to do everything for me." She described her decision to get married for her parents' sake as "going with the flow [顺应潮流]," meaning doing what other people do in a society where marriage remains nearly universal.

The desire to repay their parents was so strong that several lesbian women I interviewed were either seeking a gay man for nominal marriage, or xinghun, or had already gone through the process. Yubo, who was in a stable same-sex relationship, was active in several online groups to find a potential partner for a nominal marriage. Yubo was adopted by her family at a young age. The previous year, her parents bought her a condo, a decision that upset her brother, who suggested out of jealousy that their parents should count on Yubo for old-age support. Her relatives seemed to disapprove of the "overgenerous" move of her parents and started gossiping about her family. Yubo suddenly felt she was under tremendous pressure to do whatever she could to live up to her parents' expectations: her parents not only spent a large portion of their savings on her home but also sacrificed their relationships with her brother and other relatives. In addition to protecting parents from gossip, nonheterosexual leftover women like Yubo feel a strong sense of obligation to give their parents a grandchild, one of the reasons many lesbians are seeking xinghun. Nonheterosexual women's reluctance to come out to parents, as I discuss in chapter 4, contributes to their lack of interest in advocating for legal recognition of same-sex marriage and child-bearing outside marriage in mainland China.

I want to end this section with a quote from Lan mama, an activist and volunteer at PFLAG China who had extensive experience talking to parents of queer individuals.[47] "Giving parents a grandchild is the most important part of filial obligation and cultural common sense," Lan mama acknowledged, referring to the efforts of lesbians and gays to live up to parental expectations. She then pointed out the problem of Chinese intergenerational relationships: "Chinese adult children place too much emphasis on parental expectations. We cannot assume that all filial children have good relationships with their parents. Filial children and their parents usually do not communicate effectively because those children dare not express their real desires." As I show throughout this book, the lack of equal and effective communication between the two generations, as well as daughters' desire to meet parental expectations and protect their parents from gossip and loss of face, prompt them to tailor their strategies to deal with legal constraints in a way that allows them to fulfill their obligation as a filial daughter.

CONCLUSION

Over the years, media coverage and research studies have depicted parents as leftover women's "enemies" who push their daughters into marriage merely because of their conservative, traditional, and backward beliefs; leftover women, on the other hand, are considered victims of the resurgence of gender inequality and patriarchal cultures in China.[48] This is a misinterpretation of intergenerational relationships in leftover women's families. It turns a blind eye to the support Chinese parents are willing to provide to their daughters, as well as the gratitude leftover women have for their parents.

What I saw again and again in my fieldwork was both generations' willingness to prioritize family interests over individual desires. Parents are eager to fulfill their obligation by helping their daughters find a marital partner and taking care of their grandchildren. The strategies adopted by leftover women's parents are not always appropriate, but it is not necessarily unreasonable for parents to expect their daughters to get married and have children as soon as possible, considering the political, legal, and social environment they live in. It is possible that their health may decline as they age, making grandparenting tasks difficult to fulfill. It is also stressful to deal with inquiries about whether and when their daughter is going to get married, as well as criticisms of their failure as parents to help their daughter solve the "problem."

This chapter discusses the pattern of parent-child interactions based on guilt in Chinese families and how it puts pressure on leftover women to get married and have children. It is leftover women's emphasis on their filial obligation and the resulting sense of guilt that make the feelings of parents so influential. Going back to the question of why leftover women cannot simply ask their parents to "shut up and leave them alone," we have learned that leftover women are driven by a sense of guilt to live up to parental expectations. Indeed, since the strict implementation of the one-child policy in the early 1980s, the younger generation has become the focus of the family, with the downflow of family resources being a key feature of Chinese intergenerational relationships. This chapter, however, cautions against translating this downflow of resources into the decline of patriarchal power and parental authority in intergenerational relations in China.

The Chinese state's commercialization of housing and privatization of childcare in recent decades have pushed family members of different generations to rely on one another.[49] According to Anqi Xu and Yan Xia's study, "Chinese families as a lifeboat have become even more important than ever for family members."[50] This is especially the case when purchasing homes and finding affordable and reliable childcare are extremely difficult for the younger generation, who tend to be overworked and underpaid in China. The younger generation's dependence on their parents for housing and childcare support, as well as the sacrifices parents have made for their children, becomes a justification for parents to intervene in their adult children's marriage and childbearing, as well as the younger generation's perceived moral duty and filial obligations to live up to parental expectations. These changes have in fact reinforced the power imbalance between the two generations, resulting in the prioritization of parental expectations over leftover women's individual desires.

At the same time, the importance of the entire family working together to handle everyday challenges further reinforces the belief that family members should prioritize the needs of the family and suppress individual desires. As Xu and Yan note, "Family collectivism and mutual dependence are preferred over individualism and continue to be the dominating family values."[51] What matters most for family members is to help one another navigate the complexities of statist and repressive laws and policies, social bias and discrimination, lack of affordable childcare, and financial difficulties. Individual desires, let alone the communication between the two generations about personal desires that are potentially in conflict with the survival and well-being of the family, become secondary considerations. Going back to the metaphor of Chinese families as lifeboats for family members: the immediate danger pushes all family members to cooperate and fight together to survive, leaving little space for individuals to emphasize personal desires that may cause internal conflict in the family.

CHAPTER TWO

Relation-Based Legal Consciousness

My first interview with Lufang was on a hot and humid summer evening at a boutique café in her neighborhood. She took a seat, took a deep breath, and immediately launched into her story of rushing into marriage to fulfill her filial obligation. As the story went on, she focused exclusively on parental expectations, so I asked whether her decision was also influenced by the media campaign against leftover women and other people's opinion about her leftover status. "I could not care less about the media campaign and gossip about me among my relatives and neighbors. Sadly, those things had stressed out my parents tremendously. They were very anxious when I was single," Lufang answered, her gaze fixed on the fine bone china coffee cup in front of her. After another deep breath and a few seconds of silence, she continued, "To start with, I don't owe anything to those people. Relatives, neighbors, and other people around us are irrelevant to my personal life, and they don't necessarily have good intentions when they are talking about my situation. Some of them just don't have better things to do with their lives, and some of them enjoy getting involved in matchmaking. My pressure was from my parents."

Lufang was one of many Chinese women who told me they did not care about gossip but were either considering or had already entered a marriage for their parents' sake. If not for their concerns about parental expectations and interests, leftover women like Lufang would have been able to remain relatively unaffected by social stigma. However, social stigma affected these filial daughters' strong sense of obligation to protect their parents from gossip, criticism, and shame, as well as their feeling of guilt when they fail to do so. The negative impact on their parents makes it extremely difficult for leftover women to ignore what the media and other people say about their status.

Another determining factor in Lufang's decision to rush into marriage was related to childbearing, as she could sense that her parents wanted a grandchild badly. Lufang told me, "They kept saying that it would be difficult to have children if I waited for too long and that I should do it as soon as possible for the sake of my health." Lufang herself preferred not to have children because of the possibility of long-term health problems caused by childbirth such as low back pain and depression. However, she felt that as the only child of parents who worked very hard to give her an education and housing, she should at least take their feelings into consideration and have one or two children as soon as possible. The law against childbearing outside marriage made rushing into a marriage almost the only option for Lufang, as violating the law would likely mean losing her job.

Three decades of implementation of the one-child policy in China has significantly reinforced the sense of obligation among Chinese daughters to get married and have children in order to carry on the family line and protect their parents from social stigma and gossip. Being the only child of the family and receiving unconditional financial support from parents also comes with a sense of obligation to live up to parental expectations and protect family interests. The impact of social stigma and gossip is enormous, and it has discouraged many leftover women from forgoing a heterosexual marriage or becoming single mothers by choice.

Being a single mother in China remains highly stigmatized, despite increasing interest among leftover women in having children on their own. Chinese society tends to label single mothers as immature and irresponsible women as they have not considered the impact on the children, their families, and society.[1] The social stigma attached to single mothers is so prevalent in Chinese society that some leftover women themselves support the law's denial of unmarried women's reproductive rights. They consider the lack of legal recognition of single motherhood a necessary mechanism of deterrence that keeps single women from engaging in sexual relations outside marriage, especially those who have little money and education. Some women even suggest that the Chinese state should promote greater awareness of the punishment for having children outside marriage. Nevertheless, leftover women's attitudes tended to shift significantly when I asked what they thought about single women who were financially and emotionally well prepared to become single mothers by choice. In such cases, evading the law by accessing assisted reproductive technology services overseas or turning to illegal services in mainland China did not seem to be a big deal.

In this chapter, I draw on feminist relational theory, existing studies on relational legal consciousness, shared reality theory, and critical analyses of Chinese families and interpersonal relationships to develop the concept of relation-based legal consciousness to help us make sense of leftover women's compliance with the law, evasion of the law, or manipulation of the law. Relation-based legal consciousness is a process whereby an individual constantly picks up signals from the broader community and interaction with her close ones to construct her version of the close ones' expectations and develop strategies to deal with the law accordingly. This process relies heavily on the leftover woman's own interpretations of the information based on her specific situation.

When a leftover woman is constructing her perception of parental expectations and developing her strategies to deal with legal barriers, she must simultaneously refer to the broader community's expectations regarding (1) how a responsible citizen should relate to the law; and (2) what a filial daughter should do for her parents. Factors such as financial status, dependence on parents for support, and sexual identity all play a role in shaping the broader community's expectations at both levels. Understanding leftover women's choices from the lens of obligations helps explain why many of them still prioritize parental interests in the absence of emotional intimacy between the two generations. The emphasis on obligations also points to the need to define "close relationship" more broadly to include the individual's obligations in the discussion of the impact of our relationships on our legal consciousness.

It is my hope that by calling for more attention to the impact of the sense of obligation, relation-based legal consciousness can provide a new perspective to capture the relational nature of legal consciousness in a way that highlights our social embeddedness through our obligations. To this end, this chapter starts with definitions of "relation-based" and the "relational self" before it engages with studies on the impact of relationships on legal consciousness to advocate for a more nuanced definition of "close relationships." It then draws on debates over the relational formation of legal consciousness and the co-construction of meanings to illustrate how the broader community's expectations affect us in our close relationships.

TOWARD RELATION-BASED LEGAL CONSCIOUSNESS

As Lynette Chua and David Engel suggest, all legal consciousness research is and has always been relational.[2] In fact, relational theory has become a hot topic in the social sciences, the humanities, and legal studies, which lays the foundation for an in-depth discussion of the relational nature of legal consciousness from different perspectives. Not surprisingly, relational rights and the relational nature of legal consciousness have attracted growing attention from law and society scholars in the past decade.[3] Some scholars build on feminist analysis of the relationship between law and autonomy to discuss legal consciousness in North America and beyond, while others take a different approach and focus on non-Western societies and communities "where the influence of Enlightenment philosophy was uneven and popular understandings of atomistic individualism had shallow roots."[4]

To understand leftover women's legal consciousness in the broader context in Chinese society and the distinct patterns of parent-child interaction in Chinese families, I borrow from Shuming Liang, who describes Chinese society as a relation-based society. Liang argues that Chinese society is neither individual-based nor society-based but relation-based: it focuses on the particular nature of relations between individuals who interact with one another rather than on any particular individual.[5] According to Liang, people in a relation-based society often understand the relationship between society and the individual, as well as the relationship between individuals, from the perspective of their obligations within the society rather than their rights as an individual.[6] For example, it is common for parents to tell their child that it is their obligation as parents to provide the child with a good education, but it is unlikely that the child will insist that it is her right to ask her parents to pay the tuition fees. In other words, Chinese society stresses the need to fulfill one's own obligations first and achieve rights by relying on other people's fulfillment of their obligations.[7] Building on Liang's work, Ambrose Yeo-chi King argues that people in a relation-based society interpret the nature of a particular individual's behavior in terms of how it fits or fails to fit the interpersonal standards of society and culture.[8]

I use the term "relation-based" to describe leftover women's legal consciousness in order to emphasize the powerful influences of obligations in addition to emotional intimacy on our legal consciousness and call for more attention to the multiple layers of obligations of a particular individual. Relation-based legal consciousness aims to capture the process during which the relational self understands the law and decides how to engage with the law based on her evaluation of her obligations as an individual within her family, her social groups, and the broader community.

Relation-based legal consciousness reveals the inherent hierarchies of layers of obligations in shaping legal consciousness, depending on the "closeness" of these relationships. It emphasizes that the sense of closeness cannot be narrowly defined as emotional intimacy that involves effective and transparent conversations and communications between the two parties; rather, it also involves the individual's moral obligations to another person within her family and social networks.

The concept of relation-based legal consciousness benefits greatly from relational theory and relational legal consciousness scholarship, which taken together reveal the relational nature of the self and the law's power in shaping relationships, the impact of relationships on our legal consciousness, and the co-construction of meanings and reality among individuals. I now draw on these scholarly debates to discuss the key elements of relation-based legal consciousness.

The Relational Self

As Lufang emphasized throughout the interview, her decision to rush into marriage was because of pressure from her parents more than anything else. She mentioned several times that she could not be selfish and think only of her own preferences because her parents supported her education and housing unconditionally. Her strong sense of obligation to repay her parents and her sense of guilt motivated her to get married and have children. Lufang would not have to care about the illegality of childbearing outside marriage if not for her parents' desire for a grandchild. As ignoring the feelings and interests of her parents was not an option for Lufang, focusing on the law's impact on her individual rights without putting intergenerational relationships front and center leads to misunderstandings of her legal consciousness.

As feminist relational theorists powerfully argue, conventional liberal rights theories and the individualistic and rationalistic conceptions of the self and autonomy fail to capture our relationships with the law.[9] Individualistic conceptions are problematic in that they do not make relationship central to the understanding of the human subject.[10] Feminist relational theorists advocate for a relational conception of the self that "recognizes not only that we live in relationships with others but also that relationship and connection with others is essential to the existence of the self. The human self in this view is constituted *in* and *through* relationship with others. We define ourselves *in* relationship to others and *through* relationship with others."[11]

The central idea of feminist relational theory is that "individuals are situated in networks of relationships in and through which they are co-constituted within the broader social framework of institutions and norms."[12] To feminist relational theorists, relationships of power and oppression are "nested in and shaped by relationships at familial, community, national, and global levels."[13] Given that law is one of the chief mechanisms of structuring human relations, these scholars emphasize the law's power in shaping our relationships. Jennifer Nedelsky writes, "Law is a powerful means of structuring human relations, and it is also an important way in which concepts like self and autonomy take shape in the world."[14] Similarly, Martha Fineman's vulnerability theory challenges the dominant conception of the universal legal subject as autonomous and independent individuals and emphasizes that people are inevitably embedded beings who are dependent on social relationships, institutions, and structures.[15] Fineman argues that our current system fails to reflect the vulnerable and dependent nature of human condition, and she advocates for the replacement of the reasonable man of law with the concept of embodied vulnerable subject.[16] In particular, she calls for attention to how social institutions privilege and protect some while tolerating the disadvantage and vulnerability of others, thereby producing and exacerbating existing inequality.[17] Law, for example, structures relations in ways that undermine equality and autonomy.[18]

By revealing the relational nature of the self and autonomy, feminist relational theory has offered inspiration to law and society scholars to go beyond the "overly individualistic framework" in legal consciousness scholarship.[19] As Chua and Engel point out, "If the self is essentially relational, it follows that an overly individualistic framework will fail to capture the essence of her legal consciousness."[20] Over the past decade, the concept of the relational self, among other contributions of feminist relational theory, has been influential in shaping our understanding of the impact of the law on individuals and their relationships, as well as their perceptions of and engagement with the law. For example, Engel discusses how Nedelsky's theory of the relational self and Fineman's vulnerability theory point to the need to challenge the myth of the autonomous self in the United States and stresses the powerful role of interpersonal connections in shaping injury victims' decision making regarding whether or not to claim rights.[21] Most recently, in the presidential address at the 2023 Law and Society Annual Meeting, Laura Beth Nielsen referred to Nedelsky's analysis of relational autonomy to develop her concept of relational rights, which Nielsen defines as "a way to think about the law that emphasizes, values, privileges and protects important social relationships."[22]

Feminist relational theory's emphasis on relationships helps us understand the connection between leftover women's choices and the law that regulates Chinese family structures and relationships in a way that disadvantages these women. The law's denial of childbearing outside marriage eliminates the possibility for Lufang and many other leftover women to fulfill their filial obligation to give their parents grandchildren legally. To make things worse, the implementation of the one-child policy has made daughters like Lufang the only hope of their family and reinforced their belief in the need to continue the family line.

The broader context in which Lufang and many other leftover women make decisions regarding marriage and childbearing, however, is different from Anglo-American societies where the liberal conception of the self as autonomous and independent prevails. Throughout history, the self has always been highly relational in Chinese cultures and can only be defined within and through relationships. This relational nature has also been reflected in laws and policies in China, ranging from the one-child policy to legal constraints during the COVID-19 pandemic.[23] Most importantly, many leftover women and parents hold a negative attitude toward the concept of autonomy in the context of marital choices, with some of them equating an individual's emphasis on autonomy with being selfish and self-centered. When I asked Lufang how she thought about her decision to get married and have children, she explicitly said that it was not an autonomous choice and that there was a lot of pressure from parents and parents-in-law. However, she immediately suggested, "I don't think autonomy is among the most important values in Chinese society. Being autonomous is somewhat too selfish and willful, which may hurt the feelings of our parents."

The narrative of Chaoying, a twenty-eight-year-old construction estimator in Putian, further illustrates leftover women's concern about prioritizing autonomy in the context of Chinese families. She said, "Autonomy is more about financial and intelligent independence. When it comes to marriage and childbearing, however, the family, rather than the individual, is the most basic unit in Chinese society. I don't really think we need to follow whatever our parents tell us to do, but the harmony of the family trumps autonomy. To me, marriage is not only the union between the couple but also between two families."

To understand the relational self in Chinese society, I now turn to Xiaotong Fei's renowned theory of the "differentiated mode of association [差序格局]."[24] According to Fei, the construction of Chinese social relations is based on social networks of personal relations with the self at the center of each network, with family members often occupying the circles closest to the center. Fei describes the network of relationships in Chinese society as an egocentric pattern similar to the concentric circles formed when a stone is thrown into a lake and each circle spreading out from the center becomes more distant and at the same time more insignificant.[25] Fei emphasizes the word *tui* (推), which means "pushing out" or "extending out," in the sense of ripples expanding from the center. The process of tui, according to Fei, always starts from the self and spreads out from the center gradually to the relatively more and more distant people within her network of connections.[26] Depending on how far the individual pushes out, her scope of social connections can extend to include countless people from the past, present, and future.[27]

Fei's analysis of tui captures the hierarchy of relationships in shaping leftover women's legal consciousness. When leftover women are evaluating how they should understand and engage with the law during the process of tui, they usually start from the closest relationships and gradually extend to the more distant to look for answers. They first look to family dynamics, interdependence, and the health status of their parents, among other things, to evaluate their obligations. However, as parents do not usually express their expectations directly, leftover women must go one step further and consider what other people within their family's social networks may think. The importance of referring to what other people think also lies in the fact that those people's comments have the potential to significantly affect the women's parents and family reputation. Referring to other people's expectations to figure out what works best for her family and parents is a process that relies heavily on assumptions and presumptions, during which leftover women must also look to the broader community's collective expectations to find out the socially acceptable ways to understand and engage with the law to better make sense of the rationales for what people within their social networks expect.

The relational self in Chinese society, therefore, is arguably more relational than the relational self that has been described in feminist relational theory. This highly relational nature of the self as embedded in layers of relationships and expectations highlights the need for a more nuanced analysis of the closeness of our relationships to better understand their impact on our legal consciousness.

The Impact of Close Relationships
on Legal Consciousness

Because of the prevalence of the social stigma attached to single mothers in Chinese society, most leftover women are reluctant to challenge their parents by initiating a discussion about the option of becoming a single mother. Yiyue is a twenty-seven-year-old clinical laboratory technologist working in a public hospital in Putian, a relatively conservative city in eastern Fujian province where patriarchal thinking prevails. She suggested that entering a heterosexual marriage in Putian often means "downgrading the quality of life" because wives are expected to be submissive and take on all the housework even when working full-time. Through her work, Yiyue got to know the nuts and bolts of the legal requirements for assisted reproductive technology service, and she was critical of the law's denial of unmarried women's reproductive rights. Despite her support for single mothers and her desire for children, Yiyue was reluctant to have children outside marriage because of her concern about her father's reaction. "My father would beat me to death if I dared to give birth outside marriage," Yiyue said.

Yiyue's reluctance to break the law to pursue an alternative family structure had little to do with whether she agreed with the law. Rather, it was about her concern that she would not gain acceptance from her father and would therefore damage her family relations. The importance of family relations in shaping our legal consciousness has been documented in several studies in the past decade. Writing on law and immigration, Leisy J. Abrego demonstrates that the legal consciousness of family members of undocumented migrants about citizenship status is highly relational and develops through key mechanisms within the family.[28] According to Abrego, "Family proves to be a key site for the social and relational production of citizenship because while all members of society may help inform citizens' legal consciousness, the narratives, expectations, untold fears, and limiting experiences of loved ones most prominently played a role. At the core, then, U.S. citizen members of mixed-status families develop a legal consciousness based on lived experiences of privilege, responsibility, and guilt—and all of these are rooted in the love they feel for their families."[29] Abrego's study reveals that love within a family, as well as the sense of guilt or debt, significantly shapes the legal consciousness in the household. It demonstrates that the narratives and experiences of loved ones, especially those who are targeted by harsh laws and enforcement practices, are the most powerful in informing citizens' legal consciousness.[30] In addition, in her work on the impact of the Deferred Action for Childhood Arrivals in the United States, Abrego shows that legal changes that affect individuals usually end up shaping the legal consciousness of their entire families: it makes family survival easier, instills greater collective confidence in meeting family goals independently, and leads to a greater sense of belonging in the United States.[31]

At the same time, Hsiao-Tan Wang's influential article, "Justice, Emotion, and Belonging," powerfully demonstrates how the sense of being included or excluded by family members as *zijiren* (自己人) determines whether or not one sues family members for lawful interest.[32] *Zijiren* is loosely translated as "one of us" or "group insider."[33] According to Wang, the sense of zijiren is "a culturally embedded emotional complex of belonging that refers to a psychological classification schema of one's level of relational inclusivity or exclusivity within a given group."[34] Wang suggests that family members may ignore the tension and avoid disputes in order to maintain the feeling of zijiren.[35] Building on Wang's work, my previous research on legal consciousness under the one-child policy discusses how the sense of zijiren encourages collaboration among family members and close relatives to evade the law and how our responses to the law change significantly when we situate ourselves in different types of relationships.[36] These studies have captured the significant impact of close relationships on legal consciousness, revealing how they shape our identities and perceptions of the law.

Engel's study of injury victims' reluctance to claim rights in the United States and Thailand offers a deeper analysis of the rationale behind the relational self's motivation to take into account significant others' perceptions during the process of understanding her relationship with the law. Drawing on shared reality theory, Engel suggests that people collaborate in their construction of the understanding of the world in which they live, especially with those who are important to them.[37] Engel writes:

> When there is a strong motivation to preserve the relationship over time, then the version of reality they generate is more likely to endure. For injury victims, this means that interactions with their closest friends and family members will produce a shared understanding of the accident, why it happened, and what should be done about it—and this understanding is likely to have a powerful effect on the victim's thoughts and actions for quite a long time, because of the strength and stability of the relationships.[38]

The powerful impact of close relationships on our legal consciousness, in this sense, results directly from our desire to maintain a sense of closeness and belonging, as well as the importance of the exchange of love, gratitude, emotional intimacy and support, and care.

While shared reality theory is merely one of many theories Engel has engaged with in his analysis of the legal consciousness of injury victims, it helps explain why close relationships affect us more than distant ones. "Shared reality" is the product and experience of the motivated process of having in common with others' inner states about the world.[39] The term "reality" refers to people's *subjective* perceptions of something being real and trustworthy.[40] What has been shared is a commonality in people's inner states, including their beliefs, judgments, feelings, or evaluations concerning a target reference such as a particular politician or religious issue.[41]

A primary contribution of shared reality theory to legal consciousness studies is its discussion of social tuning, especially through interactions with significant others. During the process of creating shared reality, "people take into account the views of others, especially significant others, to appraise experiences and events, and to construct or verify views about various types of issues."[42] According to shared reality theorists, we especially socially tune toward close others, where shared understanding matters greatly to such an extent that sometimes we confuse our significant others' expectations with our own.[43] Shared reality theorists define "significant other" as "any person who is (or has been) influential and in whom one is (or once was) emotionally invested, including family members, past or current romantic partners, friends, or coworkers."[44] Our desire to maintain relationships with significant others leads to what shared reality theorists refer to as "affiliative social tuning," which occurs "when individuals experience a desire to get along with their interaction partner and this affiliative motivation encourages the individual to spontaneously and genuinely align their attitudes and/or behaviour with their interaction partner to achieve a sense of shared reality."[45] This is why the breakdown of an important relationship tends to lead to a high level of distress: when a close or intimate relationship dissolves, the individual loses an important source of shared reality that allowed her to validate her judgments, feelings, and opinions.[46] When it comes to leftover women, the breakdown of intergenerational relationships is unthinkable: as described by Fei's theory of differentiated mode of association, the self is defined in her network of relationships in a way that family relations enjoy the highest priority.

To understand the role of affiliative social tuning in shaping leftover women's construction of parental expectations, it is crucial to underline that leftover women define "close relationships" in a broader sense than closeness based on emotional intimacy that comes from the sharing of thoughts and feelings with another person in a safe, equal, and trusting way. To be specific, leftover women emphasize the importance of fulfilling their obligations in addition to and sometimes even instead of intergenerational intimacy; and in many cases, there is little communication between leftover women and their parents about the former's desire and the latter's expectations. To some extent, leftover women and their parents are "close" in terms of moral obligations within their family and social networks rather than emotional intimacy. This emphasis on obligations enables us to understand how leftover women participate in creating shared reality without much communication with their parents. While an individual's love for her family is subjective and intangible, obligations of a particular individual are often easier to define because they are largely co-constructed by the members of the broader community.

Yiyue's explanation of her reluctance to violate the law reveals the nuanced differences of closeness. When I asked her why she came to the conclusion that her father would beat her to death without finding out how he really felt, she explained that she knew for sure there was no way her father would agree. Yiyue described her father as someone who "has never been present or involved in the lives of his two daughters but still wants to have a say on our marriage and childbearing to ensure the family's continuity and reputation." In fact, it is common for the mother to take on the sole responsibility of nurturing the next generation in Chinese families, while the father is usually not very involved in the upbringing of his children.[47] Nevertheless, the father often tends to be the one who cares more about the family's reputation and the one who wants to have a say in their children's life-changing decisions such as marriage and childbearing. Many leftover women describe their fathers as "a familiar stranger under the same roof," meaning that they do not really know each other deeply.

Yiyue was one of many leftover women born in the 1980s and 1990s in rural Fujian whose fathers went to a nearby city for work and sent money home to support the family. These women spent little time with their fathers and found it difficult to articulate what a father's love meant to them. As Evans points out, "Many of these fathers were often absent from home on work, and their daughters frequently described them as 'authoritarian,' 'dictatorial' and 'patriarchal' figures who tolerated little challenge to their authority from either their wives or their daughters."[48] However, daughters still feel a strong sense of obligation to defer to their fathers for their major life decisions. While it may be true that leftover women are emotionally closer to their mothers, it is usually difficult for Chinese mothers to confront their husbands in order to protect their daughters. Thus, the father's insistence on the interest and reputation of the whole family often pressures leftover women to comply with mainstream norms. For Yiyue and many other leftover women in this situation, the motivation to appease their parents by following the traditional path of having children within a heterosexual marriage comes from a sense of filial obligation rather than love and emotional intimacy between the two generations based on genuine conversations about their desires and needs.

Very few leftover women I interviewed chose to step outside their comfort zone to initiate conversations with their parents about alternative family structures. Among those who had the nerve to do so, the importance of maintaining family relations ended up making it extremely difficult for them to negotiate with their parents—after all, they must resort to affiliative social tuning in their conversations in a sensitive way. Mincong, a twenty-six-year-old who worked as a nurse in a maternity-care center, dared not attract attention to herself by engaging in any conversations with her parents about her sexuality. But she was among the brave ones; she tried to seize opportunities to figure out her parents' attitudes toward same-sex relationships without putting herself under the spotlight.

A few years ago, Mincong was shopping with her mother and saw a lesbian couple kissing in the shopping mall. Seeing it as an excellent opportunity to learn her mother's attitude, Mincong asked her to look in that direction. She tried her best to not seem too excited about the scene and did not make any comment, as she had no intention of attracting attention to herself. All she said was, "Mum, look, there is a lesbian couple." Mincong's mother immediately expressed her disapproval by accusing the lesbian couple of ignoring their parents' feelings. Mincong remembered vividly the comments made by her mother: "Do their parents know? How devastating this would be for their parents if they saw this. Have the girls ever thought about their parents' feelings?" Since then, Mincong made up her mind to never confront her mother with her sexuality, assuming that there was no way her mother would accept her queer identity. I wonder whether Mincong's mother would have adopted a different tone if Mincong said something to support the lesbian couple, but it was clearly far too risky for her to challenge her mother at that time. As the only child in her family, Mincong did not think it was an option to hurt her mother's feelings due to the social stigma attached to homosexuality. Mincong said, "The society is too young and immature to accept my sexual identity."

Mincong's decision to never discuss it again with her parents was both a product and a reflection of the existing social stigmas and the broader community's expectations regarding how and what a filial daughter should do to prioritize the interests of her parents. Most queer women in China chose to completely avoid discussion about their sexual orientation with their parents. At the time of my fieldwork in 2016, only 5 percent of China's

70 million LGBTQ people were out of the closet; the rest lived invisibly.[49] According to George Radics, "Although homosexuality is not illegal in China . . . heteronormative expectations of marriage and children, along with strong filial piety expectations, force LGBTQ people to hide their feelings and prioritize social obligations over individual desires."[50]

During my fieldwork, the majority of heterosexual leftover women used the term "normal" (正常) to refer to their sexual orientation when I collected demographic information. Only when I probed further into the meaning of "normal" would they define it as "being attracted to the opposite sex." While the reasons for their reluctance to use "heterosexual" directly to answer my question may vary, their use of the term "normal" indicates the stigmas attached to sexual minority populations in Chinese society and heterosexual women's strong desire to draw a clear line between themselves and queer women. To be fair, this does not necessarily mean that they were opposed to homosexuality. Rather, their purpose was to emphasize that they were not part of the LGBTQ community.

When leftover women sense that their parents may be strongly against their desire to have children on their own or form a same-sex partnership, they avoid inviting conflict between the generations. This is especially the case when leftover women cannot predict how their parents would react to these topics and how it could potentially damage their family relations. In other words, leftover women usually do not feel comfortable communicating with their parents about alternative family structures in a social and cultural environment that stigmatizes single mothers and queer women, nor do they think they should.

Only through the lens of obligations can we better understand how "close relationships" shape leftover women's legal consciousness when there is tremendous social pressure for the family to ensure every family member lives up to social norms. For many leftover women, the pressure to get married and have children is closely related to their sense of indebtedness resulting from the support they have received from their parents over the years. The downflow of resources from parents to the young has further intensified the sense of guilt in leftover women who delay or forgo heterosexual marriage. The emphasis on the individual's obligations embedded in her family relations and social interactions makes it difficult for the leftover woman to communicate with her parents directly about their preferences and desires in a "young and immature" society. As a result, leftover women must draw on whatever information they have in order to figure out and construct their versions of parental expectations.

The Construction of Leftover Women's Perceptions of Parental Expectations

The stories of Yiyue and Mincong demonstrate that their strong sense of filial obligation and the lack of opportunities for effective communication between the generations discouraged explicit conversations about their personal desires. It may well be the case that most such women are not sure about what exactly their parents think, let alone want to negotiate with them. Instead, leftover women construct a version of parental expectations on their own to guide their development of strategies to deal with the law's denial of their right to alternative family structures. They make assumptions based on the signals they have picked up from daily interaction with their parents, other people around them, and the media, during which process they also participate in shaping and reshaping their parents' attitudes and the broader community's expectations.

Recent studies on the relational formation of legal consciousness have demonstrated that people become co-creators of legal consciousness through their social interactions.[51] In her 2014 study of the Hawaiian cockfight, Kathryne Young uses the term "second-order legal consciousness" to describe "a person's beliefs about the legal consciousness of any individual besides herself, or of any group whether or not she is part of it."[52] Young's study makes the crucial point that our legal consciousness is not only influenced by our own experience but also by our understanding of others' experiences with and beliefs about the law. In a more recent article, Young and Hannah Chimowitz emphasize that second-order legal consciousness "operates as an ongoing, interactive set of social processes through which existing power relations are produced and reproduced."[53] Young's second-order legal consciousness has sparked scholarly interest in how fraud investigators' understanding of the legal consciousness of welfare clients shapes their enforcement tactics, as well as how the latter's legal consciousness is shaped by that of the former.[54] These studies demonstrate the interplay between the legal consciousness of the two sides and the ongoing back-and-forth in each side's assessment of the other.

This co-construction of legal consciousness is also occurring virtually through our interactions online and even through our interpretation of the information presented by the media. Scholarly discussion of the social construction of legal knowledge in the media can be traced to William Haltom and Michael McCann's *Distorting the Law*. Envisioning "ideology" as "definable but indeterminate cultural logics from which humans actively construct meaning and make sense of things," Haltom and McCann emphasize that the production of ideology is an ongoing interactive process that involves inviting, encouraging, privileging, and facilitating certain types of interpretive constructions over others.[55] Anna Kirkland's study of the legal consciousness of fat acceptance advocates provides a compelling example of how the media shapes mass consciousness: it reveals that the "mass cultural production of the unhealthy and morally decrepit fat person undergirds an account of what kind of person is undeserving of rights protections."[56] It is, therefore, not surprising to see many fat acceptance advocates rely on the logic of functional individualism in their reasoning about their rights.[57] In response to the ubiquitous presence of smartphones and social media platforms in recent years, Fabio de Sa e Silva uses the communication between legal agents and the public on Facebook to demonstrate the significant role of social media platforms in allowing the co-creation of shared cultural schemata on law and invites scholars to investigate further the production of legal consciousness in the digital age.[58]

The state-sponsored media campaign against leftover women since 2007, according to Fincher, has depicted single women in their late twenties and beyond as "leftover or spoiled food" and promoted the idea that children born to women over thirty would not be as healthy as those born to younger women.[59] Fincher suggests that many leftover women "genuinely believe the destructive myths perpetuated by the state media" and rush into marriage.[60] It may appear on the surface that Fincher's analysis captures Lufang's story because she was one of those leftover women who ended up rushing into marriage to get rid of her leftover status and have children as soon as possible. However, interpreting Lufang's story in this way seems hasty for two reasons. First, there is little attention paid to the ongoing back-and-forth during the interactive process captured by the discussions of the co-creation and co-construction of legal consciousness. After all, members of the broader community are not passive receivers of the Chinese state's media campaign and ideologies; instead, they participate in shaping and reshaping these ideologies through their everyday interactions with other people by accepting some components but resisting those that they disagree with, which may in turn shape the media campaign. In fact, the broader community can reject the values promoted by the Chinese state and collectively determine how to resist inequality and injustice.

Second, there is little discussion of leftover women's resistance to mass cultural production and the process during which they actively evaluate available options by taking into account other people's legal consciousness and moral judgments to evaluate their marital decisions. For Lufang and many other leftover women, rushing into marriage does not necessarily translate into their belief in the ideology prevalent in the media. Instead, it is out of their obligation to protect their parents from the negative impacts resulting from this prevalence.

During the process of constructing their versions of parental expectations, leftover women critically evaluate the signals they have picked up from the media, the broader community, and their interaction with parents in a holistic way. The media may indeed have some influence on the broader community's expectations, but members of the broader community digest the information selectively. When it comes to how an individual should deal with legal barriers, they do not necessarily buy into all values promoted in the media but instead often resist the ideology imposed from the top by developing strategies to engage with the law in creative ways to protect local norms and values. As Nadler points out, "Qualities of the law itself, including the extent to which it is perceived as furthering justice or reflecting community values, influence the extent to which people feel bound by law in general."[61]

To borrow the concept of second-order from Young, what leftover women care about most is often not what the media promotes or what the law stipulates but rather what the broader community considers appropriate ways to deal with the values and restrictions imposed from above. After all, in a relation-based society, fitting in is crucial for the prosperity and even survival of the leftover woman's family. According to shared reality theorists, creating shared reality, a process of sharing that involves the subjective experience or awareness of a commonality, allows individuals to experience a more valid and reliable view of the world, evaluate other people or groups, and at the same time obtain a sense of belonging and who "we" are and what "we" want.[62] In the process of creating shared realities with each other, our sense of closeness or "we-ness" increases.[63] To fit in and maintain relationships, leftover women must constantly participate in creating shared reality with members of the broader community by upholding the mainstream expectations that others consider crucial.

Confucian virtues and family values were among the most frequently invoked concepts during my fieldwork in the discussion of the importance of filial piety and how Chinese people should uphold these values instead of emphasizing individualism and autonomy. Fitting in requires an individual to demonstrate a sense of "Chineseness," or what Lisa Rofel refers to as Chinese "cultural citizenship" and "Chinese cultural and national identity,"[64] by fulfilling their filial obligation. Failure to embrace these values will affect an individual's reputation in her social groups. Even if a leftover woman does not feel grateful to her parents, she may still feel the need to act like a culturally appropriate Chinese citizen to gain respect among her peers, especially when people around her all assume that she has received unconditional support from her parents.

The importance of fitting in and creating a sense of "we-ness" explains the difficulties for leftover women to completely ignore the broader community's expectations—after all, their parents desire to fit in too. While many leftover women are not affected by the media campaign against them and have no intention to please relatives and neighbors who gossip about them, the influences of the broader community's expectations on their legal consciousness are inevitable, especially when they feel an obligation to protect their parents from gossip and shame. The abstraction of the broader community's expectations takes shape in the leftover woman and her parents' interaction with their neighbors, friends, relatives, colleagues, and others either physically or virtually in their everyday lives. These are people who can gossip about the leftover woman, arrange matchmaking events for her, criticize her parents for failing to find her a good match, and impose pressure on the woman and her parents to fulfill familial and societal obligation in order to fit in with the mainstream. In a sense, they can directly exercise informal social control by expressing disapproval and condemnation of leftover women's "deviance" and looking down on these women's families. Furthermore, they have access to more detailed information about the leftover women, enabling them to make specific comments about the women's obligation as filial daughters and responsible citizens.

The first level of the broader community's expectations, which focuses on how a particular individual should engage with the law to be a responsible citizen, serves as the foundation of leftover women's understanding of their relationship with the law.

They develop their strategies according to the broader community's evaluation of the law's "moral legitimacy," meaning its fit with established social and cultural norms within the society regarding right and wrong, fairness, and deservedness, as well as an individual's obligation as a respectable member of society.[65] While a law that aligns with social and cultural norms will usually be accepted by the broader community, a law without moral legitimacy does not deserve much respect.[66] In the latter situation, the broader community may tolerate and even encourage evasion of the law by a respectable individual.

The second level of the broader community's expectations, which focuses on the filial obligation of daughters and sons, tends to be less straightforward and more dependent on individual circumstances. Nevertheless, this second level often ends up setting a higher standard for leftover women as they try to figure out their strategies to deal with the law. Understanding the interaction of the two levels of the broader community's expectations is the key to making sense of leftover women's strategies to deal with the law's restrictions.

When leftover women are trying to figure out their strategies to deal with the law's denial of childbearing outside marriage, for example, they must demonstrate their efforts to be responsible citizens who understand how to engage with the law in ways that reflect the collective legal consciousness in the broader community. Those who fail to do so would put their family reputation at risk. The importance of fitting in motivates these women to take account of the broader community's disapproval of so-called immature and naive single women's childbearing outside marriage and its opposite attitude to so-called high-quality women's choices to become single mothers. In other words, leftover women must prove that they are qualified to evade the law against childbearing outside marriage according to the broader community's standard to avoid damaging their family reputation and inviting gossip. Nevertheless, understanding the broader community's collective legal consciousness is only one step of the process of constructing the leftover woman's version of parental expectations. Those who have reached the standard of being qualified to evade the law must also evaluate their filial obligation to protect their parents from the potential consequences of their "deviant" choices based on their own circumstances, which is highly dependent on their family background, financial status, and sexuality, among other factors. In other words, they must fulfill their obligation both as responsible citizens and filial daughters to ensure that their decision to choose alternative family structures is acceptable to the broader community.

As a family member's failure to live up to the broader community's expectations may affect the whole family's reputation within its social network, the leftover woman must figure out her obligation to protect her parents. It means that parents do not necessarily need to express their expectations explicitly. It is also inappropriate for parents in a relation-based society to emphasize their own rights and expectations unless it is through the lens of their own obligations. The relation-based nature of parent-child interactions helps explain why filial daughters must still tailor their strategies to deal with legal restrictions in a way that prioritizes the interests of parents in the absence of emotional intimacy and effective communication.

In fact, the broader community's expectations are so influential in leftover women's construction of their versions of parental expectations that these women may often end up reinterpreting what their parents have explicitly expressed in order to align with mainstream standards. It sometimes prevents leftover women from appreciating their parents' acceptance or tolerance of their decisions to choose a path that diverts from the mainstream. This usually occurs when it comes to the second level of the broader community's expectations: leftover women's strong sense of filial obligation may lead them to construct a version of parental expectations that goes beyond or even potentially contradicts what their parents have said. The lack of effective communication between the two generations further contributes to this tendency. I use the local practice of *lianggu*, which can be loosely translated as "taking care of both sides," to further explain this process of interpretation and construction.

A relatively new theme that emerged in my fieldwork was daughters' obligation to continue the family lineage and perform ancestor worship, both of which remain very important in Chinese society.[67] Traditionally in China, only male descendants can pass on the family name and are responsible for ancestor worship. However, this has changed as there are many families without male descendants due to the one-child policy. The idea of having a child who carries the wife's family name was brought up in all the focus groups I conducted with leftover women in Fujian. Several women suggested that the reason they decided to have at least two children was that their parents wanted one of the grandchildren to continue the family line: if a couple had just one child, it would generally be difficult for the wife's family to convince the husband's side to have the child carry on their family name; thus, a plan or promise to have two children would significantly increase the chance for the husband's family to allow one child to have the wife's last name.

In Putian, in particular, today families without sons generally expect their daughters to follow the local custom of lianggu, which requires the husband and the wife to take care of parents and children and the worship of ancestors on both sides of the lineage, not just on the husband's side.[68] Lianggu has existed in Putian for decades, but it only became a default recently when daughters born under the one-child policy reached marriageable age. Although it is a desirable practice across Fujian to have a child with the wife's family name, Putian is one of the few places where daughters without male siblings tend to buy into the idea that it is their responsibility to take care of both sides and carry on the family lineage. If the family fails to ensure that at least one daughter (particularly the elder one) is willing to practice lianggu, neighbors or fellow villagers may look down on them. As a result, even before the shift from the one-child policy to the universal two-child policy, many women evaded the law in order to have two children to achieve the goal of lianggu, some of whom were not only forced to pay fines but also lost their jobs.[69] This emphasis on lianggu under the one-child policy in Putian reflected the broader community's prioritization of its importance over compliance with the law.

Many eldest daughters of the family had a strong sense of obligation to practice lianggu without being requested by their parents to do so. This strong sense of obligation results primarily from their own desire to repay the continuing and sometimes unconditional support from their parents, as well as the broader community's expectation for them to prioritize family interests and reputation over their own freedom to choose partners and family structures.

Chenqi, a thirty-year-old environmental scientist and the eldest daughter of her family, said, "I have a strong sense of filial duty, and I know I put too much pressure on myself. But my parents work hard to accumulate financial resources to be passed down to us. I feel we should repay them by giving them a grandchild who can pass on the family name." Lianggu, however, is not easy to fulfill. Virtually all my interviewees in Putian attributed the large number of leftover women there to the practice of lianggu. This is because most men in Putian still consider it a challenge to their masculinity. The fear of losing face and bringing shame to his own parents stands between the man and his marriage if the woman's family requires lianggu.

Having seen how determined Chenqi was, I was surprised to learn that her parents did not explicitly pressure her to practice lianggu. They were busy operating a private hospital in another province, which kept them away from their hometown and the gossip about them to some extent. Her parents mentioned several times that they would be fine if Chenqi and her younger sister preferred a "normal heterosexual marriage" instead of lianggu. Chenqi's mother even told her not to bother having two children. Her father said that he would be willing to "grit my teeth and let you marry into other people's family [咬咬牙让你嫁出去]." But Chenqi insisted that following lianggu was part of her filial obligation.

When following lianggu is widely considered the eldest daughter's obligation, Chenqi and many other women without male siblings may feel a need to establish their social normality within their communities by following the practice. Driven by the strong desire to repay her parents, Chenqi prioritized her perception of what would be best for her parents over what they actually said. She might have felt that her father's reluctance, shown by his usage of "grit my teeth," was more important than his apparent approval of a marriage without lianggu. While it was up to Chenqi to decide how to interpret her father's words, her father had consciously or at least subconsciously conveyed his disappointment and left space for Chenqi to speculate about what he truly wanted. Not surprisingly, conversations between leftover women and their parents are often filled with subtle reminders like this one that push adult children to read between the lines. The stories of Yiyue, Mincong, and Chenqi demonstrate how leftover women process the cues and signals they have picked up. During the process of constructing parental expectations, leftover women must take into consideration the broader community's expectations of an individual's obligations and evaluate how their choices may affect their parents because of these expectations.

CONCLUSION

Perhaps one day, when the world is older and mature enough, leftover women will not have such difficulty communicating with their parents about alternative family structures. In the foreseeable future, however, social stigmas attached to leftover women, single mothers, and queer women will prevail in Chinese society. In this chapter, I discussed the relational self in Chinese society and one's obligations as a filial daughter in her family and as a responsible citizen in the broader community. My adoption of a definition of "close relationship" that is broader than emotional intimacy and is linked to moral obligations among significant ones calls for more attention to the impact of the sense of obligation on our legal consciousness. To capture the emphasis on one's own obligations in Chinese society, I developed a concept of relation-based legal consciousness to help us understand leftover women's perceptions of the law's denial of their access to alternative family structures and their strategies to deal with the restrictions. Central to relation-based legal consciousness is the process during which the individual picks up signals from different sources to construct her version of the expectations of closest family members when direct and equal conversations about personal desires and rights are not possible. The importance of maintaining family relations and fulfilling her filial duty leads the leftover woman to resort to social tuning, which may make it even harder for her to know exactly what her parents expect.

It may be true that those born and raised under the one-child policy already have more freedom than the older generations to talk to their parents in a less submissive and obedient manner about many things. Parents have the option to either aggressively push their daughters into marriage or adopt the subtler approach of displaying weakness. Nevertheless, leftover women do not enjoy the same level of freedom due to their obligations, given the stigmas attached to leftover women, single mothers, and queer women and the potential consequences for their parents and family reputations. After all, in a relation-based society, leftover women are not supposed to insist on their rights explicitly, especially when their parents have provided a good education and housing, among other types of support.

CHAPTER THREE

Suzhi and Parental Expectations

Lin baba, in his late fifties, was confident that he would be the most open-minded parent I would interview in my fieldwork because he was one of the very few people in his social network who supported decoupling marriage and childbearing. Throughout the interview, Lin baba emphasized that a woman who was "strong enough" (足够强大) deserved the right to evade the law and have children on her own. He kept saying it would be acceptable if his thirty-year-old daughter decided to remain single for the rest of her life as long as she had a child at some point. "If a woman is strong enough to be financially and mentally independent, marriage is not a good deal," said Lin baba. To support his view, Lin baba referred to the story of Shu Qi, who was among the highest paid actresses in China and on the Forbes China Celebrity 100 list. "Shu Qi was born in 1976 and has now reached her forties. I don't think she is concerned about her leftover status because she is strong enough," he said. Despite his open-minded attitude toward leftover women, he wanted a grandchild badly. Lin baba suggested that there were many ways for a strong leftover woman to evade the law and have children, including traveling overseas for surrogacy and other assisted reproductive technologies.

Assuming that Lin baba was open-minded and supportive of alternative family structures, I asked what he would do if his daughter went through a divorce or preferred a same-sex partnership.[1] The smile on his face suddenly disappeared. He knitted his brows and responded in an authoritative voice.

> I prefer her to be leftover over being divorced. I mean, getting a divorce is against the Chinese value of completeness and fullness [圆满]. There will be negative impacts on parents. But getting a divorce is still better than being gay. There is no way I could accept her decision to be gay. You know why? It would significantly affect my life. What if my friends and relatives knew about her sexuality? It could be much more serious than losing face. My friends and relatives would accuse me of failing to educate her well and suspect that I had some problems. I mean, like father, like son. My mental health would suffer badly if I was ridiculed in this way.

Unfortunately, given the widespread stigma attached to homosexuality in China, Lin baba's concerns are not unfounded. Although he was ahead of many parents who were reluctant to see their daughter become a single mother by choice, he was not unlike them in terms of prioritizing family reputation over the happiness and personal desires of their children. Lin baba's emphasis on having to be "strong enough" to secure resources to combat legal discrimination and challenge social attitudes and his strong disapproval of same-sex partnership are closely related to his fear of losing face and being morally judged in a relation-based society where fitting in is extremely important to his well-being and social status.

In Lin baba's view, whether a particular leftover woman could be qualified to evade the law and have children depended on if she had enough resources to prove to others that she had the capacity to take responsibility for her decisions. In fact, throughout my fieldwork, leftover women regardless of sexual preference generally considered the law negotiable as long as they had enough resources. "Laws and policies from above will always be countered by strategies on the ground [上有政策下有对策]," was a recurring theme in conversations about the law's denial of single women's reproductive rights. In general, leftover women and their parents had no respect for the law, and neither did they fear potential penalties for evading it. They mentioned various ways to evade a law that denies unmarried women's access to assisted reproductive technology services, including using cross-border reproductive care, underground reproductive services, and even conceiving using the sperm of a known donor via home insemination. Many of them held the view that their primary task was to make sure they met the broader community's expectations regarding how a responsible citizen should engage with the law rather than advocate for the right of unmarried women to have children.

When it comes to leftover women's reproductive rights, their lack of interest in fighting and even learning about the law, as we will see throughout the chapter, largely results from the broader community's emphasis on the differential treatment between "high-quality" and "low-quality" populations. The suzhi, or human quality, discourse, a political keyword officially designated in China's eugenics campaign to justify social and political hierarchies of all sorts, ended up dominating the discussion of the law's denial of leftover women's reproductive rights during my fieldwork. Ironically, as my data suggest, the reason ordinary Chinese citizens, including leftover women and their parents, invoke the concept of suzhi is to approve high-quality leftover women's right to ignore the law and have children outside marriage. The suzhi discourse and its role in justifying unequal treatment of "high-quality" and "low-quality" women significantly affects leftover women's legal consciousness. The prevalent discourse of suzhi in Chinese society, the "social maintenance fees" under the one-child policy, the high cost of assisted reproductive technology services overseas or in the underground market, and the expenses of raising children in China all contribute to the widespread belief that only "high-quality" leftover women with sufficient resources deserve the right to have children outside marriage regardless of the law.

Despite the emphasis on suzhi, leftover women with higher suzhi do not necessarily enjoy more freedom in terms of choosing alternative family structures. As Lin baba's sudden change of attitude when asked about divorce and homosexuality indicates, even if a leftover woman manages to live up to the broader community's expectations regarding suzhi to be qualified to evade the law, she must also consider the negative impact of her behavior on her parents and make sure she fulfills her filial obligations.

Leftover women's perceptions of legal discrimination against unmarried women's reproductive rights represent some common features of legal consciousness in Chinese society. First, individual members of a stigmatized group tend to stress the competition among themselves for the qualification to evade the law directly when there is little hope of gaining rights for all members who suffer from a particular type of legal discrimination through challenging the law; and imposing a law from above would not necessarily lead to significant changes for the individuals due to the broader community's expectations in terms of their obligations within their social and familial networks. Second, the relation-based society's emphasis on fulfilling one's obligations, rather than asserting rights directly, contributes to ordinary citizens' prioritization of working on improving the self to be qualified to work around the law over advocating for legal changes.

In fact, the discourse of suzhi is about the broader community's trust in the individual's ability to fulfill her obligations. Leftover women's desire to accumulate resources in order to meet the broader community's standard and be qualified to evade the law not only demonstrates the significant impact of the broader community's collective legal consciousness on their strategies to deal with legal restrictions; it also reveals how leftover women actively participate in co-constructing the broader community's collective legal consciousness. At the same time, leftover women must also attend to the broader community's expectations of filial obligations, given the cultural significance of filial piety in Chinese societies and identities.

THE MYTH OF SUZHI

Since 2015, Chinese feminist activists and lawyers have made great progress in advocating for unmarried women's rights to assisted reproductive technology services in mainland China, stirring a national debate and making it a key topic for legislative changes in 2020.[2] Nevertheless, most leftover women demonstrate little interest in challenging the law. Legal constraints on unmarried women's reproductive rights were widely considered negotiable, meaning that they would be able to find ways to work around them. The importance of having high suzhi to combat social and legal discrimination was frequently brought up by my interviewees in the discussion of whether and how to choose alternative family structures, including forgoing marriage, becoming single mothers by choice, and entering or remaining in same-sex relationships.

Suzhi is a sweeping idea that is relevant to educational background, civic values, global citizenship, family environment, the way a person talks and behaves, middle-classness, social distinction, and self-cultivation.[3] Due to the ongoing eugenics campaign, in present-day China the improvement of individuals' suzhi is considered the foundation of social stability and national strength.[4] The Chinese state also continues to use the suzhi discourse to restrict the rights of its "low-end population," a phrase that refers to poorer, less well-educated rural residents and rural-to-urban migrant workers.[5] After decades of promotion and reiteration of suzhi in television shows and newspapers, it has become a pervasive term in people's everyday conversations.[6]

In the past few decades, Chinese citizens have been invoking the suzhi discourse to divide people into the categories of high-quality (*gao suzhi*) and low-quality (*di suzhi*) citizens. On the one hand, people use "low-quality" to describe the "uncivilized" or "backward" behaviors of people from rural areas; on the other, "high-quality" is used to refer to elites and the middle class or to emphasize the need to invest in education to accumulate suzhi and ensure self-development and class mobility.[7] By portraying rural-to-urban migrant workers as low-quality people who need to build more suzhi into their bodies,[8] the discourse of suzhi justifies the need to control China's internal migration for the sake of social stability.[9] At the same time, there are ongoing campaigns of "community building" that aim to raise the overall suzhi of urban residents, which divide urban residents into those of high quality who are fit to participate in self-governance and those of low quality who are fit only to be governed.[10]

The suzhi discourse helps justify inequality embedded in the legal system and discourages less privileged leftover women from advocating for legal changes. Similar to what Michael Katz refers to as the "undeserving poor" in the United States, the broader community depicts those so-called low-quality women as not deserving of sympathy.[11] The rationale is personal failure is responsible for their "low quality" and financial condition. The stigmatization of "low-quality" women reflects both the soft and hard versions of "poverty as a problem of persons" discussed by Katz: the soft version "portrays poverty as the result of laziness, immoral behavior, inadequate skills, and dysfunctional families"; the hard version, on the other hand, "views poverty as the result of inherited deficiencies that limit intellectual potential, trigger harmful and immoral behavior, and circumscribe economic achievement."[12]

In Chinese society, being a low-quality woman is a stigmatized identity that signals personal failure and the inability to fulfill one's obligations and be responsible for one's behavior. Becoming single mothers will reinforce this stigmatization, especially when these women cannot afford the high cost of providing the best education and resources for the next generation. At the same time, people assume that "low-quality" women will pass their low suzhi on to the next generation because of their rural background, working-class identity, and lack of postsecondary education, all of which are considered related to their genetic makeup.[13] The suzhi discourse, which is part of the eugenics campaign in China's population planning policy to promote healthy birthing and childrearing and to discourage rural people from having too many children, has a close link with genetic engineering.[14] The emphasis on genetic makeup resembles the discussion of "inherited deficiencies" and Social Darwinism, which dominated the hard-core eugenics theory that justified racism and social conservatism in the United States by the 1920s.[15] Similar to the argument among behaviorists that "the 'lower class' emerged as un-American,"[16] Chinese society blames "low-quality" mothers for reproducing the next generation of undeserving "low-quality" citizens.

Unfortunately, as Erving Goffman argues, there is a tendency for stigma to "spread from the stigmatized individual to his close connections."[17] A leftover woman's underserving status is contagious within her family: as Lin baba suggested, his relatives and friends would question his capacity to educate his daughter well and even assume that Lin baba himself must have some "problems." Thus, moral worthiness and deservedness affects the whole family. Many women are more concerned about their parents' feelings, reputation, and face than their own.

In the context of reproductive rights, people generally assume that only a woman who does not have enough suzhi to understand her responsibility as a mother would have a child outside marriage. Thus, it is not unusual for them to agree that "low-quality" women's rights to have children outside marriage should be denied by the law. Huihong, a twenty-five-year-old leftover woman who worked in a public hospital, was strongly against the idea of legalizing childbearing outside marriage. She said, "It makes sense for the law to deny single women's reproductive rights—otherwise, what happens if you don't have the money to raise the child? How are you going to deal with the tremendous pressure from the social stigmas and the impact of shame and gossip on your parents?" Huihong claimed that many single women and girls did not know how to protect themselves, so the law should step in to deter them from doing "stupid" things that would invite unnecessary condemnation and gossip for themselves and their parents. Similarly, Lijun, a thirty-one-year-old architect, suggested that legal constraints served as a form of protection for single women and their children. She said, "Sexual education is lacking in China, and thus many girls do not understand what they are doing and end up having abortions. That's why I support the law's denial of childbearing outside marriage. . . . I don't think their parents can ever agree with that choice and accept the child because of public opinions and gossip."

Both Huihong and Lijun considered the consequences of childbearing outside marriage unbearable because of the potential impact of social stigma on leftover women's parents. They consider the law benevolent in that it prevents "naive" and "immature" leftover women from making choices that hurt their parents, even if protecting the interest of the parents was unlikely the law's intention. As Yunxiang Yan argues, "Family policies in China were formulated and implemented for the interests and wellbeing of the nation-state."[18] Leta Hong Fincher asserts that the Chinese state uses the media campaign against leftover women to achieve its population planning goals.[19]

Indeed, many leftover women expressed concerns about the potential consequences of allowing childbearing outside marriage because of the assumed immaturity and irresponsibility of so-called low-quality women and its impact on the suzhi of the population. Meng mama's daughter, Yun Meng, was one of them. She cautioned:

> It is dangerous to legalize unmarried women's reproductive rights all at once because of the huge gap between urban and rural women's suzhi. There are far too many unmarried mothers in rural China who have only received very limited education. The legalization of childbearing outside marriage will further encourage these low-quality women to give birth without considering whether they can support their children in the future. I mean, if the Chinese state

really wants to legalize it, we had better start with pilot projects in big cities and see how things go. Otherwise, we would have problems if rural women gave birth to too many children and did not care for them. The situation in China is different from the West, as in some areas in rural China people do not have much suzhi.

What Yun tried to emphasize was that legal restrictions must be in place to prevent rural women from "irresponsible childbearing," meaning having children outside marriage when they do not have the resources to offer the children a safe and stable environment. Her assumption is that lacking sufficient education is one of the reasons rural women give birth outside marriage without thinking through the potential impact it could have on themselves, their families, the children, and society as a whole.

Embedded in Yun's concern about the potential consequences is the presumption that rural women who give birth outside marriage tend to have little money and therefore are not responsible enough to decide to have children and fulfill their obligation as good mothers by providing a good education. Indeed, the suzhi discourse was put forward in the 1980s against the backdrop of market reform across the country. It has a strong emphasis on material and specifically economic factors.[20] As Ellen Judd's research suggests, the Chinese state considers the low quality of rural women "a problem that needs to be corrected" and thus has put forward a series of policies to raise their suzhi through education and occupational training.[21] The rationale for these policies, according to Judd, is that "women would have higher status where they produced more value, as measured directly through the value of their economic products."[22] Thus, one's earning power often translates into one's suzhi. Similarly, Ke Li writes in *Marriage Unbound: State Law, Power, and Inequality in Contemporary China* that, influenced by the suzhi discourse, it is widely believed in contemporary China that a high-quality man "is willing and ready to spend money for his girlfriend or wife," while a low-quality man "is much less inclined to do so due to moral or educational deficiency."[23]

The embeddedness of one's earning power in suzhi blurs the boundary between suzhi and financial resources in people's daily conversations about whether a particular individual deserves more rights. After all, it is up to the individual who invokes the concept of suzhi to decide how much emphasis she places on the person's earning power and financial resources when she evaluates the person's worthiness. It is, however, generally believed that anyone who has low income tends to have low suzhi. The idea resembles Katz's "undeserving poor," although the focus of suzhi is on whether the person is well-educated and well-behaved enough to accumulate financial resources.[24] The discourse of suzhi magnifies social differences by derogating rural migrant workers and encouraging people to compete and accumulate suzhi in order to have "more value than others and therefore [become] more deserving of the rights of citizenship."[25] Instead of encouraging ordinary people to think critically about the uneven distribution of educational resources, the suzhi discourse leads to the assumption that it is the individual's responsibility to improve their own situation to deserve more rights. One's failure to accumulate financial resources and educational achievements can lead to being stigmatized as a low suzhi woman who must be governed by the law more strictly. There is a lack of trust in "low-quality" women's capacity and willingness to be responsible for their own decisions in Chinese society.

In most cases, it was only when I reminded my interviewees of the existence of single mothers by choice that they would shift the focus from the "miserable lives" of underprepared single mothers to single women's right to intentionally have children outside marriage. "Single mother by choice" refers to a woman who chooses to have a child on her own, usually via adoption or some form of assisted conception, with the intention of being her child's sole parent from the outset.[26]

Lijun suddenly became supportive of the idea of becoming a single mother once she thought of it as a "choice" rather than a "consequence." She said, "I can understand why they want to have children on their own. In our industry, many female employees have the desire to do so—all of them are outstanding professionals and have bought homes and cars on their own. They don't need a marriage." Lijun's comments reveal the importance of earning power. Even if a leftover woman is well educated and well behaved, she cannot assume that she is qualified to evade the law and have children on her own unless she is confident about her earning power and has accumulated sufficient money to afford it. This is largely related to the high cost for a single woman of evading the law for a child. After three decades of implementation of the one-child policy, Chinese people tend to believe that an individual's evasion of the policy is morally acceptable as long as she can take full responsibility for her choice and avoid bringing trouble to other people.[27] It means that the individual must find a way to evade the law without negatively affecting other people and at the same time afford the social maintenance fees necessary to register the child for legal status and the other costs resulting from her decision to have a child illegally.

In the years leading up to the shift to the two-child policy, the most common penalty for violation of the policy was the imposition of social maintenance fees. At the time of my fieldwork, Ailan, an officer overseeing the implementation of the one-child policy in a residents' committee, told me that the social maintenance fee in urban Xiamen was approximately RMB 150,000 (US$20,550) for a couple who exceeded the number of children they were allowed to have if paid on time, and those having children outside marriage could be charged approximately 60 percent of this amount.

The embeddedness of one's earning power in suzhi, as well as the imposition of social maintenance fees under China's population policies, has led to the widespread assumption among Chinese citizens that if a person has enough suzhi, there are always ways to evade the law. The broader community's expectations regarding who is qualified to evade the law have led many leftover women to believe in the power of money and the importance of improving earning power to gain societal acceptance.

Leftover women generally agreed that they must pay the social maintenance fees to ensure the child's access to education and healthcare. They considered an individual's ability to pay the fee the primary factor that determined whether a couple or an unmarried individual was qualified to evade the law. In a focus group with both single and married women who used to be referred to as leftover women, the participants concluded that what prevented an individual from evading the law was usually the lack of financial resources. Kailin, a twenty-eight-year-old civil servant, started things off.

> It costs around RMB 500,000 to have one baby through surrogacy in the underground market, and another 500,000 for twins. The cost does not stop rich people from using the services. Rich couples are more than happy to pay to choose the number and sex of their babies. I think the most important task for leftover women is to become affluent. We could have as many children as we want via whatever means if we have enough money.

Indeed, surrogacy is a luxury that only the affluent can afford in China, in part because China bans all forms of surrogacy.

However, the estimated number of underground surrogacy operations nationwide exceeded twenty thousand per year,[28] and a significant number of wealthy Chinese traveled overseas to seek surrogacy services. The fact that many affluent people were seeking surrogacy services reinforced Kailin's belief that it is money that matters, not the law. To her, having more than one child and the freedom to turn to surrogacy and other types of cross-border reproductive care were goods that people could purchase as long as they could afford it.

One of the key reasons Kailin and other focus group participants felt no need to stress other aspects of suzhi further demonstrated the blurred boundary between suzhi and one's earning power, as well as the abstract nature of suzhi. In fact, I never encountered anyone who would describe herself as of low quality, nor is it common for people to use the term "low-quality" to refer to their family members, relatives, and friends. When people use the term, they are primarily referring to an abstract group of strangers they imagine to be very different and remote from themselves. The purpose is to disqualify the "underserving" strangers from enjoying certain rights.

Leftover women's emphasis on financial resources also stemmed from the high cost of raising a child. China is the second most costly country in the world in which to raise a child to the age of eighteen, with the cost being 6.9 times the gross domestic product per capita.[29] A 2022 report suggests that the average cost of raising a child to adulthood in urban China can be almost US$100,000, which is more than the cost of raising a child in Japan and the United States.[30] The suzhi discourse, unsurprisingly, contributes to this high cost. It is a widely shared sentiment among parents that "you should not let your child lose at the starting line [别让你的孩子输在起跑线上]," emphasizing the importance of offering the best education to ensure they grow up to be high-quality citizens.[31] According to Teresa Kuan, author of *Love's Uncertainty*, middle-class Chinese parents hope that investing in their children's education will confer stability over the long term.[32]

This widespread assumption that a high-quality woman with sufficient financial resources is qualified to evade the law and have children on her own has motivated many leftover women to work hard to accumulate financial resources for the freedom to have children outside a heterosexual marriage. Ideally, Wei would like to establish a family with a close woman friend who shares the same interests and values and have one to two children. But she stressed that the only way to achieve this goal was to work hard to get a promotion and salary increase. This was her strategy to protect her parents from gossip: "If I have a very successful career, my parents can talk about my achievements and busy schedules to explain why I have to forgo or delay a heterosexual marriage."

In fact, "path-paving" (铺路) as a process of accumulating enough suzhi in preparation for coming out is a recurring theme in existing studies on nonheterosexual individuals' marital choices in Chinese societies.[33] Path-paving, according to Shuzhen Huang and Daniel Brouwer's research, refers to "a process whereby, by preparing oneself through quality living and financial success, the queer subject also prepares their parents and others to better respond to the difficult, disruptive speech act of coming out."[34] To many of their interviewees, only those with high-quality living standards and who fall within the category of successful members of society are qualified to think about coming out.[35]

This is also evident in the discussions about the denial of same-sex marriage and the resulting lack of access to assisted reproductive technology services for LGBTQ people in mainland China. When asked about her attitude toward legal discrimination against nonheterosexual individuals, Yanping, a small business owner who self-identified as queer, shook her head and told me she could not care less about the law: "I don't feel I am affected much by legal discrimination. I believe that as long as I work hard to make sure I have a lot of money, I can have a good life. Money can do everything and solve all problems, and laws and policies will no longer matter once you are affluent."

Deng Jie, a volunteer leader of PFLAG China, stressed that LGBTQ activists and researchers in China should not overemphasize the importance of "rights," a view consistent with Timothy Hildebrandt's finding that LGBTQ people in China believed the legal recognition of same-sex marriage would do little to improve their lives.[36] Deng Jie clarified, "If a lesbian or a gay wants a child, she can hire a surrogate through the underground market. It is illegal, and so what? There are so many illegal things happening every day in China. But people still find lots of ways to get those things done underground.... Some people just go to Hong Kong or the US for surrogacy if they can afford it."

The widespread belief in using money to navigate legal constraints has motivated many leftover women to focus on improving their own financial and social status to deserve more rights rather than advocate for equal treatment and the universal right to have children outside marriage. Proverbs such as, "With enough money, you could even hire a demon to drive your mill [有钱能使鬼推磨]" and "If a problem can be solved with money, it is not a problem at all [钱能解决的都不是问题]," were so prevalent in my fieldwork that I felt I was asking the wrong question when I brought up legal discrimination against unmarried women's reproductive rights. When the discourse of suzhi is so influential in dividing people into those who deserve more rights and those who only deserve to be governed, it is understandable for leftover women and their parents to place so much emphasis on having resources to be qualified to evade the law.

DEFLATING THE MYTH

If Chinese society and parents agree that high-quality women have the right to evade the law and have children outside marriage, why do we only see a small number of high-quality women become single mothers by choice? Why are LGBTQ people with privileged backgrounds reluctant to have children outside a heterosexual marriage? To answer these questions, more attention needs to be paid to the formation of relation-based legal consciousness: given the impact of the broader community's expectations on individual families in a relation-based society, it is reasonable for leftover women to believe that the most important thing they can do to fight the law's denial of unmarried women's reproductive rights is to accumulate sufficient financial resources to gain the broader community's acceptance of their evasion of the law. Nevertheless, they must consider much more than merely accumulating suzhi due to the very fact that the broader community not only expects her to be a responsible citizen, but also a filial daughter.

In fact, an affluent and well-educated leftover woman who meets the broader community's expectations of suzhi may still be reluctant to have children outside marriage once she turns her attention to potential gossip and disapproval from people around her and the impact it will have on her parents. To further complicate the situation, leftover women from affluent and powerful families are often held to a higher standard as many of them are considered role models within their social networks and communities.

I want to draw on the stories of two affluent leftover women to discuss how the broader community's expectations of filial daughters may turn out to hold high-quality women to a higher standard. Among all the leftover women I interviewed, only two, Linying and Hangyan, had seriously considered the option of having children on their own and researched how to get it done in and outside mainland China. Not surprisingly, they happened to be among the most affluent and well-connected women I had encountered in my fieldwork. Linying's parents had achieved great success in transnational businesses in several industries, while Hangyan was a civil servant whose parents were highly influential politicians in Fujian. At the time of the interview, Linying was single. Hangyan had already married and took part in my research to walk me through how she decided to enter a marriage despite her initial preparation for single parenting. I chose to focus on the two most privileged women among my interviewees not only because of their confidence in navigating legal restrictions but also because neither of them ended up going down the "deviant" path.

When I met with Linying in 2016, she was two years into her job at one of the top financial companies in Fuzhou, a dream job for many. Her privileged, well-connected family not only paid for her master's degree at an elite university in North America and helped her secure the job but also provided resources for Linying to feel confident about evading the law. At that time, Linying had spent four years trying to find someone to start a family with but to no avail. Her backup plan was to become a single mother by choice. She believed that if her parents really wanted a grandchild, then "it is better than nothing," even if having a child on her own was not ideal. Linying did not have a strong desire for children, but she decided that she should have two children just to fulfill the expectations of her parents and bring some happiness to the family. With resources and education, Linying was confident that she could easily meet the broader community's expectations regarding suzhi.

When I asked what she thought about the legal constraints on single women's reproductive rights in China, Linying shrugged it off and said, "The law in this country does not affect me much. I am a permanent resident of Canada where it is legal to do so." She then asked me whether I had ever heard of people hiring surrogates in North America and immediately said that she would prefer surrogacy over giving birth to the child herself because "if you have already paid that much for assisted reproduction, why don't you pay a bit more and hire a surrogate?"

Hangyan had a very similar understanding of her relationship with the law and its discrimination against her rights. Coming from a family with power and financial resources, she was confident that she could evade the law by getting things done outside mainland China. She said, "I was pretty serious about freezing my eggs as a backup plan just in case my Mr. Right never appeared. My initial plan was to go to Taiwan to get it done if I remained single at the age of thirty-five, although I suspected that I would not be able to use the eggs in Taiwan unless I got married. So I was thinking about Cambodia and the US as well." In addition to possibly accessing her family's financial resources, Hangyan was optimistic that her family's power and influence could help her evade the law in one way or another. She believed it was a matter of "whether you want to do so or not."

> People usually assume that civil servants cannot evade the population policy, but I have heard tons of stories of them evading the law

even when the one-child policy was strict. Some of them registered their children under their relatives, and others bribed a doctor to fake a disability certificate for the first child so they could have a second child. I mean, those so-called verified disabled children are all super smart and healthy. For civil servants, evading the law is easy breezy.

Nevertheless, although both Linying and Hangyan were well-educated and equipped with enough money to resort to cross-border reproductive care and pay the fine for evading the law, they decided to compromise and enter a not-so-ideal marriage. As of this writing, seven years after the initial interviews, Linying is childless and going through the process of getting a divorce, and Hangyan is a married mother of two girls.

Linying recently contacted me for some information about choosing to become a single mother by choice in Canada, as once again she has been considering seeking assisted reproductive technology services overseas. Three years after the initial interview, Linying picked a man who checked off almost all the boxes on her mother's list, despite her concerns about the conflict of personalities. Linying's mother had a very particular standard for what she meant by "a good match": the man should have a similar family background, have been born and raised in Fuzhou, be tall and good-looking, and have a decent and stable job. Linying always knew that he was not a good fit, but she was afraid of missing the opportunity to marry a person her mother approved of.

Despite her confidence about finding ways to evade the law, Hangyan rushed into marriage at the age of thirty-four after her mother had to quit the square dance group due to gossip about Hangyan's leftover status, a story related in chapter 1. Hangyan was not satisfied with her husband at all, as the man's family background and all other aspects of suzhi were at most average.

According to Hangyan, "The very fact that I married into his family must have made all his family members grinning so hard all the time that they could even wake themselves up at night [娶到我，他们家做梦都会笑醒]."

Given that both women did not end up evading the law despite being qualified to do so at the level of meeting the broader community's expectations, we must reexamine the widespread assumption that accumulating suzhi is the solution for leftover women who are considering having children on their own. It is true that if leftover women have the capacity to be responsible for their choices when the broader community is indifferent or even supportive of their evasion of the law, they do not care much about the legal constraints. Unfortunately, at the end of the day, the idea of accumulating suzhi is at best a placebo and at worse an illusion and even false hope for many leftover women: it manages to meet the broader community's expectation of a responsible citizen who responds to the law in a way that reflects the individual's understanding of and respect for the collective legal consciousness; however, being qualified to evade the law does not guarantee the freedom to become a single mother by choice. In addition to the evaluation of the individual's legal obligations, the broader community also assesses her filial obligation based on her specific circumstances when it comes to family structures. More importantly, parents have their expectations too, which can differ from one individual to another and is determined by the individual's position within their family and social groups, as well as the individual's resulting familial and social obligations. Even if parents are reluctant to articulate their expectations explicitly, leftover women have the obligation to figure out what they may expect based on their family backgrounds.

Linying's and Hangyan's privileged family backgrounds could come with higher expectations from their friends and relatives for these women and their families to be role models, given that they had more resources to secure a decent life. Linying's mother's high standards for her potential son-in-law reflected the family's pressure to ensure the continuity of family success and reputation to maintain their social status within their networks of connections: if Linying ended up marrying an ordinary man from a less privileged family, other people would consider it a failure of Linying's family. Hangyan's mother would have been more tolerant of gossip if she had not always been the person who enjoyed the highest levels of respect as an influential politician before her retirement. When she was trying to process the feelings of losing power after stepping down, Hangyan's failure to secure a marriage only added to her sense of losing face.

Counterintuitively, leftover women from poor rural families often express more confidence in handling parental expectations and maintaining family relations, although they do not necessarily have the resources to evade the law and have children on their own. Coming from a poor family in an isolated mountainous area of Fujian, Qiaoyu, a lead architect in Xiamen, recognized the difficulties for her to have children outside marriage due to the high costs involved. However, Qiaoyu was under far less pressure than Linying and Hangyan to enter a heterosexual marriage. Her parents did not want to annoy her, since they needed her financial support; in addition, she had gained some respect from villagers for providing support to her parents.

To put Qiaoyu's family background into perspective, her mother was a "child bride" (童养媳) brought to her father's family at the age of seven to be a future daughter-in-law. In the old days, having a child bride was a common practice in Qiaoyu's village:

parents in other poorer villages sent their daughters to Qiaoyu's village for adoption as child brides because it was relatively better off. To her parents and other villagers, having an office job in the city and a car to drive back to the village equated to a successful life. Qiaoyu significantly exceeded that standard: she had a high income even compared to most women in Xiamen, which allowed her to regularly send money home and buy gifts for her parents and brothers.

Qiaoyu attributed her freedom to remain single until the age of thirty-one to her ability to support her family.

> It makes a huge difference when you are financially independent. It is going to be a totally different story if I depended on my parents financially until this day—the pressure to marry would be enormous. Now, even though I am single, my parents and brothers must respect me and ask for my advice whenever they make big decisions. This is because I have been financially supporting my parents as much as my brothers do, if not more. Villagers don't dare to humiliate my parents too, because no one in our village can rely on a daughter like this.

Among the younger generation of fellow villagers, Qiaoyu was the one with the highest level of education and highest income, as well as the one who provided the most material support for parents. Qiaoyu made sure to let her fellow villagers know that she had a very nice life when she visited by wearing high-end clothing and accessories. "In rural China, if you have a decent life to prove your high quality, village fellows dare not look down on you too much or bully you," said Qiaoyu. She also emphasized that her parents benefited a lot from her leftover status because her money would otherwise be spent on the next generation or buying a home. Also, receiving such significant financial support from their daughter had gained them face and respect in the village, since it was interpreted as her parents' success in nurturing the younger generation.

The stories of Linying, Hangyan, and Qiaoyu demonstrate how the law's denial of unmarried women's reproductive rights affects leftover women with different backgrounds in unequal ways. On the one hand, even if a leftover woman has the resources to be considered qualified to evade the law according to the broader community's standard of suzhi, she still faces barriers to carry it out because of her obligation to maintain the family's reputation and keep her parents from "attacks" by other people. Gossip about leftover women and disapproval of their alternative family structures within their network of connections shape leftover women's understandings of and engagement with the law. Leftover women's parents and their everyday lives are significantly affected by the comments and attitudes of their relatives, friends, and neighbors—even members of their dance groups. Parents' unpleasant conversations with other people about their daughter's leftover status may give rise to anxiety and even depression.[37] On the other hand, leftover women who do not have the confidence to be qualified to evade the law sometimes end up having more freedom than those with privileged backgrounds.

CONCLUSION

Leftover women's and their parents' emphasis on improving suzhi and accumulating resources to evade the law reflects a common attitude toward the relationship with state law in Chinese society, which is the foundation of the broader community's collective legal consciousness when it comes to a piece of law that lacks moral legitimacy: when people have little respect for the law, those who have the capacity to stand out in the competition and manage to accumulate more resources deserve more rights and are qualified to evade the law.[38] Influenced by this prevalent attitude toward the law's denial of unmarried women's reproductive rights, leftover women believe that making sure one has the resources to be qualified to evade the law is more important and realistic than challenging the legal system as a whole. With social status and financial resources, they believe they can easily get approval from the broader community to ignore the law and turn to cross-border reproductive care or underground services to have children outside marriage.

When it comes to childbearing outside marriage, the broader community's emphasis on an individual's suzhi is centered on moral worthiness and deservingness. From Lin baba's emphasis on being "strong enough" and some leftover women's endorsement of cross-border reproductive care, we have seen the broader community's approval of high-quality leftover women's right to evade the law and have children outside marriage. At the same time, there is a prevailing disdain for low-quality leftover women and an assumption that they do not deserve the right to evade the law due to their inability to fulfill their obligations. From Yun's concern about so-called low-quality women's irresponsible childbearing to other women's endorsement of using the law to deter immature and naive women from giving birth, it is evident that people do not trust low-quality women and suspect that their decisions may create a burden for society and the nation-state.

This chapter discusses how the broader community's co-construction of one's deservingness to evade a law that lacks moral legitimacy shapes leftover women's legal consciousness. It also reveals the disproportional impact of the broader community's collective legal consciousness on so-called high-quality and low-quality leftover women. The stories of Linying, Hangyan, and Qiaoyu, however, help deflate the myth of suzhi by revealing the fact that a more privileged background does not necessarily translate into more freedom to choose alternative family structures. It may be true that high-quality women with financial resources can easily live up to the broader community's expectation regarding who counts as a responsible citizen by proving their capacity to take responsibility for their choice of an alternative family structure. Unfortunately, the supremacy of the interests of parents and family relations usually makes it difficult for those women to enjoy their privilege and have children outside marriage.

Leftover women's emphasis on suzhi also illustrates that the Chinese state's promotion of the suzhi discourse to justify social and political hierarchies does not always achieve its initial goals once it reaches ordinary citizens, who interpret and reconstruct its meanings. It may be true that the suzhi discourse has successfully discouraged so-called low-quality women from having children outside marriage due to the broader community's disdain for women from rural backgrounds and lower incomes. Nevertheless, it has never been the intention of the Chinese state to encourage high-quality women to forgo marriage and have children on their own. We have seen that the meanings reconstructed by the broader community matter much more than the intention of the Chinese state in shaping leftover women's choices.

Focusing on the formation of relation-based legal consciousness gives us a better understanding of the reasons leftover women and their parents have little concern about the law's denial of unmarried women's reproductive rights. While the suzhi discourse was originally employed in China's eugenics campaign with an aim to improve the country's population quality, ordinary Chinese citizens end up using the term "suzhi" to show approval for high-quality women's decision to ignore the law and become single mothers by choice and deny the reproductive rights of so-called low-quality women. The suzhi discourse diverts attention from the law's role in reinforcing injustice between married and unmarried individuals in Chinese society and blames the so-called undeserving individuals for their failure to be considered qualified to evade the law.

Some liberal social scientists may argue that leftover women who refuse to fight the law should be responsible for their own lack of "the will and organizational capacity to attack the sources of their exploitation and degradation."[39] Some people may consider Chinese leftover women and their parents too selfish to be involved in civic engagement and social movements to challenge the law for all unmarried women. Nevertheless, once we take the difficulties of fighting the law in authoritarian regimes into consideration, we can understand that their decision to prioritize accumulating resources over challenging the legal system is based on their careful evaluation and realistic understanding of all available options within the legal and political environment in China.

As Sida Liu powerfully suggests, given the limited space for liberal ideas since the early twenty-first century, Chinese citizens have learned to refrain from engaging in politics and instead focus on economic prosperity and personal well-being.[40] According to Liu, they have mastered the art of playing ostrich.[41] We witnessed a strong echo of this view in the stories of Lin baba, Kailin, Wei, and Linying. People's emphasis on suzhi and being qualified to evade the law reveals the society's respect for those who have the capacity to achieve their goals despite legal constraints. This explains why there are many leftover women who believe that working hard to get a promotion and salary increase can buy them more freedom in terms of choosing alternative family structures.

In the next chapter, we turn to stories of those leftover women who have few illusions about accumulating resources to be qualified to have children outside marriage, with a focus on nonheterosexual women. The situation for nonheterosexual women is far more complicated than that of their heterosexual counterparts because of the law's denial of same-sex marriage and the stigmatization of LGBTQ individuals in Chinese society. As Lin baba pointed out, this stigma can spread to the leftover woman's family members and can severely damage the family's reputation. In this situation, nonheterosexual women turn legal constraints and the law's silence about homosexuality into opportunities to protect their parents and family reputations.

CHAPTER FOUR

Manipulating the Law for Its Imprimatur

Sitting in a small and dimly lit café in a run-down shopping mall on a weekday evening, Mincong, the twenty-six-year-old nurse who decided not to come out to her parents, lit one cigarette after another while sharing her stories with me. She started by apologizing for smoking in front of me and, before I could tell her not to worry about it, immediately explained that she had to rely on cigarettes to keep her mind clear. Mincong was introduced to me by Yubo, a lesbian woman I interviewed earlier in my fieldwork, who suggested that an interview with Mincong would help me understand why so many nonheterosexual individuals in China are looking for xinghun, a marriage arrangement between a gay man and a lesbian woman.[1] Mincong's willingness to open up to me immediately, as I would soon find out in the interview, primarily came from her sense of pride as a filial daughter who chose xinghun because she prioritized the interests and reputation of her parents over her own desires.

"I had been in a same-sex relationship for five years before I got married to a man. There were many reasons, but it was mainly because I realized I wanted to fulfill my filial obligation as the only child of my family and to be able to have children. A marriage helps me achieve those goals," Mincong said, then pressed the cigarette to her lips and exhaled another cloud of smoke. She stared into space for a few seconds and continued, "I plan to have two children in the next two to three years or so. After that, I'll be ready for a divorce."

"What is your plan after leaving your marriage? Any expectation for your future family structure?" I asked.

"Two kids and a dog. Having a same-sex partner would be nice, but in any case, I prefer not to reveal my sexual identity to my parents. I mean I could live with a woman without telling others we are a couple," Mincong responded.

I could not help but wonder how the legal proscription of unmarried women's reproduction and same-sex marriage affected her decision to get married with a plan to get out of it. So, I asked her about her attitude toward legal discrimination and constraints for queer women.

Mincong did not seem to be interested in discussing legal discrimination. She emphasized that she would be qualified to ignore the law as long as she had money. Mincong said, "I am focusing on career development and making money now rather than actively attending any LGBT social events or spending time dating a same-sex partner. I think I am not ready yet. I must first make sure I am financially capable of providing for my future partner. I always want to be the one who takes care of my girl. I want to be able to afford whatever she wants." Mincong waved her cigarette in the air as if striking it against an invisible whetstone. "When my knife is sharp, I will go and fight my way out for a new life."

Mincong's emphasis on sharpening her knife resonated with the heterosexual leftover women I interviewed who emphasized the importance of accumulating resources to evade the law in a society where the suzhi discourse is highly influential. However, her strategy significantly differed from those who evaded the law overtly via cross-border or underground reproductive care: she "obeyed" the law and entered a legally recognized marriage to buy herself time to accumulate resources. By going through the legal process of getting married, Mincong secured a shield that protected her from the gossip and stigma attached to leftover women and nonheterosexual individuals. This shield was extremely important for Mincong's career and family reputation. In addition, a heterosexual marriage also gave her the right to have children legally, which she considered a crucial part of her filial obligation as the only child in her family. Her strategy to deal with the law was softer and subtler than the strategy of turning to cross-border or underground reproductive care. Mincong did not do anything illegal. Neither did she need to accumulate resources for the legal consequences of violating the population policy— after all, her marriage was recognized by the law. But embedded in Mincong's decision to make use of a heterosexual marriage was her disagreement with or at least her ignorance of the law's objective to push ordinary citizens into marriage for social stability and harmony. Like Mincong, many nonheterosexual individuals in China enter a heterosexual marriage with a plan to get out of it so they can enjoy the rights and benefits that otherwise would not be available.

Xinghun serves as an excellent example of the primacy of parents' and the broader community's expectations in shaping the ways in which people understand and relate to the law. This chapter not only continues the discussion of leftover women's lack of interest in fighting the law to obtain rights for alternative family structures but also demonstrates how some women actively invite legal obligations by entering a heterosexual marriage. While chapter 3 focused on the relatively more straightforward approach of legal evasion through cross-border reproductive care and underground reproductive services, this chapter aims to offer a detailed analysis of queer leftover women's manipulation of the law for its imprimatur to meet the expectations of parents and the broader community. This analysis enables a better understanding of the marginalized population's lack of interest in challenging legal discrimination and mobilizing the law in Chinese society. At the same time, it reveals the struggles and emotional costs experienced by marginalized populations under the surface of legal compliance.

We will see that those who opt for xinghun manipulate the law by first pretending to show respect for the law and then betraying it once they have achieved their goals of benefiting from its imprimatur. To queer leftover women, having a legally recognized marriage assists them in various ways: it allows them time to accumulate resources for alternative family structures, live up to parental expectations and fulfill filial obligations, secure a shield to protect them from social stigma and discrimination, and gain the right to have children legally. The prevalence of xinghun among nonheterosexual individuals highlights the relation-based nature of their legal consciousness. To be specific, choosing xinghun is largely a result of the process of relational thinking based on a woman's obligation to her family and community: for most nonheterosexual individuals, the main purpose of practicing xinghun is to please their parents and protect them from the gossip and social disapproval of those within their social and familial networks. Many of these nonheterosexual individuals have never had a chance to confirm what their parents really expect them to do and negotiate with their parents before making the decision to enter a xinghun. Their perceptions of parental expectations regarding how they should engage with the law mainly come from their analysis of the expectations of the broader community and other people around them. The stigma attached to homosexuality and single mothers in Chinese society dilute nonheterosexual individuals' interest in advocating for the legalization of same-sex marriage; at the same time, the attitudes and gossip of people around them and from their families further reinforce the sense of obligation to follow the "normal" path of entering a heterosexual marriage in order to fit in and protect the family reputation. All these expectations contribute to the difficulties of candid and effective conversations about sexuality between the two generations, forcing nonheterosexual individuals to gauge how to balance their desire for nonheterosexual relationships and their filial obligations.

The stories of Mincong and many other nonheterosexual women who chose xinghun remind us of the fact that not everybody considers evading the law overtly via cross-border or underground reproductive care the best strategy to deal with legal constraints, even if they agree on the importance of suzhi and financial resources. My discussion of nonheterosexual leftover women's resistance to the law through manipulation aims to facilitate a better understanding of this manipulation of the law in a soft but powerful way. I discuss why and how nonheterosexual leftover women look for xinghun in a relation-based society and an authoritarian regime. I then explain how their manipulation of the law for its imprimatur makes sense in a social and legal environment with limited exit and voice options.

MAKING SENSE OF XINGHUN: FAMILIES AS SITES OF BELONGING

The practice of xinghun is like staging a performance that requires attention to each detail, which involves tremendous pressure. It takes time and effort to identify a reliable partner and reach an agreement about childbearing and housing arrangements, among other things. Xinghun, as Elisabeth Engebretsen notes, "seeks to resolve intense marriage pressure by faking marriage."[2] Nonheterosexual leftover women who turn to xinghun and go through the legal process of registering as a couple with a man use the law to make a relationship without romance look "real" for parents and others.

At the same time, there are usually agreements between the two parties to counter the law's imposition of default obligations on a legally recognized couple. Some xinghun parties sign formal prenuptial agreements to prevent disputes when it is time for a divorce. Those who do not rely on a legal agreement to protect them from being taken advantage of by their xinghun partner usually have oral agreements regarding childcare, housing arrangements, wedding ceremonies, and old-age support for their elderly parents. Unfortunately, in many cases, conflicts and disputes between the two parties soon appear, leading to the breakdown of the relationship and even resentment and revenge. My interviewees affiliated with PFLAG China suggested that the majority of xinghun couples would eventually end up outing the other party to their families.[3]

Why does xinghun still appeal to nonheterosexual women and prevail in Chinese society when the process is extremely risky and emotionally demanding? To make sense of this, we must understand how xinghun works, why queer leftover women consider a legally recognized marriage important, and what benefit they expect from the process of getting married and then divorced. As Mincong suggested, a legally recognized marriage comes with the right to have children, the possibility to fulfill her filial obligation, some protection from social stigma for the whole family, as well as more time to prepare for the challenging route of being in a same-sex partnership in Chinese society.

The importance of having children was one of the primary reasons nonheterosexual individuals considered xinghun. As Mincong put it, "For me, men are just for making children [男人就是为了用来生孩子的]. I don't care that much about who I'm having the child with, but I know I must have children." Xiaoning, a twenty-five-year-old insurance broker who was actively seeking xinghun, told me, "I definitely want a kid out of my xinghun, because my parents would be chasing after me for grandchildren." Xiaoning described xinghun as a long-term cooperative relationship with a gay man to share childcare duties and costs.

Yubo, the twenty-five-year-old lesbian who connected me with Mincong, was in the process of seeking xinghun herself. Her ideal partner would be someone who did not mind having a child and could provide housing: "It is like, if he has a condo, we would be able to host my parents there like a couple when they come to visit, but in reality, I could rent another place with my girlfriend. I would be responsible for childcare, and hopefully the child could live with me. I would also encourage my parents to live in the condo they bought for me in a city about fifty kilometers from here." Yubo did not think legal discrimination against unmarried women's reproductive rights had anything to do with her. She said, "I am always certain that I will have a legally acknowledged marriage, aka xinghun, with which I will be qualified to have children under the law." Her plan was to divorce once her children became old enough to understand her decision.

Both Yubo and Xiaoning explained that they would use "DIY" to conceive their children due to the cost involved and the risk of being found out by their parents if they did not give birth to their children themselves. The latter was also the reason adoption was not an option for them. Yubo said:

> There are different ways to have children with the xinghun partner, including artificial insemination, surrogacy, and DIY. Surrogacy is not very accessible in mainland China, and I have never heard of any xinghun couple going through that process. Artificial insemination costs a lot—around 10,000 yuan based on what I have heard. I would go with DIY, meaning conceiving using the sperm of my future xinghun partner via home insemination. DIY is the most popular way of doing it among xinghun couples since it is affordable.

When I asked Yubo whether she would request her xinghun partner to undergo medical examination at a fertility clinic or a hospital to rule out a infectious disease or a genetic disorder, she said, "I don't think people go through those processes. You just gotta be careful about it and trust your choice. Make sure you don't find a xinghun partner who goes to nightclubs a lot. These are things you can tell by talking to them."

All three women also relied on xinghun to fulfill other aspects of filial obligation, in addition to having children. Nonheterosexual individuals in China, according to Susanne Choi and Ming Luo, "aspire simultaneously to satisfy respectability norms and carve out the space to pursue personal goals" rather than simply choose to comply with one or the other.[4] Engebretsen's study on xinghun identifies two key elements of what queer individuals consider "good" strategies for alleviating normative pressures: reticence or tacit expression of difference and not overstepping boundaries that preserve social harmony.[5] Xinghun stands out as a good strategy that enables nonheterosexual individuals to fulfill their familial and social obligations: they do not need to confront parents by initiating conversations on their sexuality, and they live up to parental expectations by fitting in and meeting the social expectations of the broader community.

One of the most frequently mentioned benefits of xinghun, according to my interviewees, is to avoid coming out to one's parents and causing them shame and disappointment. To some extent, the prevalence of xinghun and the lack of interest in advocating for the legalization of same-sex marriage in mainland China result from the unbearable consequences of coming out for the nonheterosexual individual and her family. Almost all nonheterosexual women I interviewed suggested that they would not choose same-sex marriage even if the Chinese state legalized it, primarily because of their parents. According to Mincong, "It is simply too risky to come out to parents unless you can afford losing them. I wouldn't even touch the subject of sexualities with a ten-foot pole. I have no idea how they would react." Yubo's concern was similar: "I don't like the feeling of not being able to control the situation. I cannot predict what coming out to my parents would lead to. If they say no and threaten suicide, I will probably still have to choose a heterosexual marriage."

Hongping, a twenty-six-year-old bisexual woman in Fuzhou who had been in a same-sex relationship for seven years, said:

> I will never let my parents know my sexuality. I know their bottom line. I am not confident that they would be able to accept it, and thus, I see no point in creating such a risky situation. Even if the law says

yes to same-sex marriages, I still won't do that to hurt my parents. I should respect them and avoid destroying family relations. If your parents would like to see you married, you got to do it for them through performance.

Hongping's narrative captured how the difficulty of communicating with parents about their sexuality discouraged many queer women from even thinking about the legalization of same-sex marriage.

As Qingfeng Wang suggests in *Self-Accepting but Not Coming Out*, coming out to parents in China often leads to the breakdown of family relations and forces parents to cover up their child's sexuality to protect the family's reputation.[6] This breakdown comes with unbearable consequences for many nonheterosexual leftover women due to intergenerational emotional bonds and material interdependence resulting from the one-child policy.[7] The so-called low-quality queer women, in particular, will be hit harder by the breakdown of intergenerational relationships because their biogenetic family is usually their primary source of financial support and sense of belonging.[8]

The fear of losing the sense of belonging to one's family and being rejected by parents is the primary reason for the prevalence of xinghun in Chinese society. As Shuzhen Huang suggests, "In a family-oriented society like contemporary China, family is a critical network where the exchange of social resources comes into existence; it is also the site where discipline, control, and oppression take place."[9] The family is so important that it becomes "the primary site of struggle among Chinese queer subjects."[10]

At the same time, there are ongoing debates among Chinese nonheterosexual individuals regarding whether it is morally and culturally appropriate to come out to parents. The best way to protect their parents, according to virtually all the queer woman

I interviewed, was to remain in the closet.[11] Some were genuinely concerned about the mental well-being of their parents. Luxia, a primary school teacher who identified as lesbian, was strongly against the idea of coming out to one's parents. I connected with Luxia through a heterosexual man who met her at a matchmaking event arranged by Luxia's colleague at the primary school. Luxia came out to the heterosexual man the second time they met to "avoid hurting someone who seems to be honest and kindhearted." But she would never reveal her sexual identity to her parents. She knew they would have to help her keep the secret while feeling ashamed and stressed, which was the last thing she wanted to impose on them.[12] Luxia framed the idea of coming out to parents as "putting parents in the closet." She explained, "If I come out to my parents, they would keep thinking about what they have done wrong and blaming themselves for not guiding me well. What's more, they would feel confused about what to say and how to act in front of others to keep the secret. We cannot put them in the closet this way."

As Lisa Rofel suggests, given the importance of harmonious relationships with parents and the risk of bringing shame to the family, those who come out to their parents may be accused of being selfish by their peers.[13] According to a Chinese gay man interviewed by Rofel, "It is wrong to tell your parents. This is not part of Chinese culture. We Chinese must look after our parents and not bring them so much grief. . . . It is selfish to think only of yourself. Perhaps that kind of thing works elsewhere, but not here in China."[14] Wah-Shan Chou, author of *Tongzhi: Politics of Same-Sex Eroticism in Chinese Societies*, contends that the discourse of rights is rather weak in resolving conflict in the familial context and stresses instead the importance of familial-cultural identity and advocates for replacing "coming out" with the strategy of "coming home."[15] According to Chou, "coming home" refers to "bringing one's sexuality into the family-kin network, not by singling out same-sex eroticism as a site for conceptual discussion but by constructing a same-sex relationship in terms of family-kin categories."[16] Coming out translates into leaving the family for sexual freedom, while coming home means covering queer desires in order to maintain close family ties.[17] Indeed, in Chinese society, the strategy of coming home is considered by many queer individuals more culturally appropriate than coming out.[18]

Cautioning against romanticizing the approach of coming home, Huang and Daniel Brouwer's research identifies a third approach between coming home and coming out, which they refer to as "coming with," to capture the reticent homophobia that represses and disciplines queer individuals in Chinese families.[19] The coming-with approach "combines the preservation of space for one's queer sexuality with tactics that stay with the family either by cultivating parental harmony or actively interrogating heteronormative family structures."[20] According to Huang and Brouwer, xinghun characterizes the coming-with approach by affirming both sexuality and family, as queer individuals manage to preserve space for queer sexuality without coming out to their families.[21] Indeed, xinghun is widely considered a better strategy than coming out among Chinese nonheterosexual individuals and is seen as "an ideal compromise between personal desire and social and family duty."[22]

Despite the fact that most of my interviewees who chose or were considering xinghun had not come out to their parents, it is common for queer individuals whose parents are aware of their sexuality to use the law's imprimatur to protect themselves and their parents from gossip and disapproval within their social networks. Some parents even take an active part in the process.

Members of PFLAG China had encountered quite a few parents who attended their events with the aim of finding xinghun for their gay and lesbian adult children. Choi and Luo's research documents how sometimes xinghun is a performance staged jointly by parents and their queer children to "answer to the demands of the wider community and maintain the family's respectability within it" and to avoid being constantly questioned by their relatives, friends, and neighbors.[23] They put forward the concept "performative family" to explain this collaboration between parents and their queer adult children.

Sunlei, a lesbian in her mid-thirties, recalled that her parents pretended that they did not know about her sexuality and kept urging her to find a male partner even though she had come out to them when she was in her early twenties. Sunlei suspected that her parents were in denial, but at the same time, "there was no way to wake up those who pretend to be asleep [叫不醒装睡的人]." Similar experiences have been documented in other studies on the experience of coming out to parents in China.[24] When Sunlei entered xinghun in her early thirties, she was not sure whether her parents truly believed her performance. The only thing she knew was that her parents were thrilled to see her marriage certificate and wedding, which to them mattered much more than anything else. It was the emphasis on reticence in Chinese family relations that enabled the "success" of Sunlei's xinghun.

When delaying and refusing heterosexual marriage translates into one's failure to fulfill filial obligation and social expectations, coming out to one's parents is unthinkable to many nonheterosexual individuals. The difficulty of having effective conversations about sexuality between the two generations contributes to the prevalence of xinghun. Furthermore, given the tremendous social pressure of fitting in faced by parents in their everyday interactions with people around them, some parents prefer their children to at least get married once, as they "believe that having a divorced grown child is less stigmatizing than having a child who has never married and is 'stuck' in lifelong singlehood."[25] Xinghun, therefore, serves as a temporary solution: manipulating the law for its imprimatur, nonheterosexual leftover women can at least put together a performance to protect their parents from social pressures.

MANIPULATING THE LAW FOR ITS IMPRIMATUR IN A RELATION-BASED SOCIETY

Throughout my interview with Sunlei, she emphasized the need to put together a performance to gain social recognition for herself and her parents. Sunlei said:

> My parents are respected figures among their relatives, friends, and colleagues. They are leaders at their workplace. It is necessary for me to protect their public image and help them maintain social recognition. I mean, if I did not get married, people would look down on them. Before I entered xinghun, my parents kept reminding me that the daughters and sons of their colleagues and friends had already been married, divorced, and remarried [都结婚结了两遍了], and I still had nothing. It sounded better to be divorced than never married. I feel sometimes we must consider the needs of our parents.

By entering xinghun and putting together a wedding banquet for her parents to invite people within their social networks to celebrate together, Sunlei felt that she had at least fulfilled her filial obligation and sustained her family's reputation by meeting the broader community's expectations and preventing gossip.

Sunlei's then-girlfriend, Zhuzhu, who accompanied her to the interview, was supportive of her xinghun. Zhuzhu found the photos of Sunlei's wedding banquet on her phone to show me. I saw Sunlei in a traditional red Chinese wedding dress, standing close to a man with pale skin. The photo was taken by Zhuzhu, who was there to support Sunlei during the wedding ceremony. I considered asking Zhuzhu why she decided to attend the wedding and how she felt at the ceremony, but I ended up joining Zhuzhu in admiring Sunlei's amazing curly hair and makeup in the photos when I realized there was a shadow of sorrow behind Zhuzhu's smile.

Sunlei managed to gain more than just peace of mind from this arrangement. At the time of the interview, Sunlei and Zhuzhu rented an apartment together in Shanghai, while Sunlei's "husband" spent most of his time in Hong Kong. Her parents no longer pestered her with phone calls about her marital status. A legally acknowledged marriage had created some room for her to be herself in the private space and brought some other benefits. Sunlei said, "I am satisfied with how I balance my private and public lives. I manage to make my parents happy and prove I am 'normal' in front of my colleagues. And I am finally eligible to buy an apartment in Shanghai because the law disqualifies single women who are not originally from Shanghai from purchasing homes." In my follow-up conversation with Sunlei in 2020, she told me that she had already gotten everything she needed, divorced her xinghun partner, and moved to her employer's central office in another city. A xinghun provided her with legal and social recognition of "normalcy" and some privileges exclusive to married couples.

Nonheterosexual leftover women's decision to enter a legally recognized marriage with a man may seem to indicate their respect for the law and willingness to follow the law. It may also appear that they have to enter a heterosexual marriage because they are "caught" or "trapped" by the law. It is problematic, however, to categorize xinghun as compliance with the law. In fact, their purpose is to go through the legal process of getting married and then divorcing to gain approval from parents and other people, as well as rights only available to married couples such as having children legally. Their choice undermines the law's intention to promote heterosexual marriage and constrain childbearing within marriage for social stability and population control. To some extent, Sunlei and other queer women who chose xinghun were in fact using the law to tear apart the ideal of the harmonious society that promotes marriage. Entering xinghun to get a divorce inevitably contributes to the increase in the divorce rate in China.

Instead of seeing xinghun as a sacrifice nonheterosexual women make to please their parents and comply with the law, I consider it a powerful but soft means of small resistance, which I refer to as legal manipulation. As of this writing, ordinary citizens' manipulation of the law has attracted little attention from law and society scholars.[26] The strategy of "following" the law to live up to expectations within one's family and the broader community deserves more attention from legal consciousness scholars, as legal manipulation by ordinary citizens has the potential to undermine the objectives of the law. This creative use of the law helps us understand people's lack of interest in legal mobilization either within or outside the formal legal system. Queer leftover women's superficial compliance with the law helps them obtain the rights denied by the law and gain approval from parents and the broader community.

Based on my interviews with nonheterosexual women, I identified two key factors that contribute to the individual's legal manipulation: the invisibility of their marginalized identity under the law and the lack of both exit and voice options.[27] First, when the law is ambiguous and even silent about certain marginalized identities, it unintentionally leaves some space for an individual to achieve the goal without legal consequences. Second, the simultaneous lack of both exit and voice options further motivates the individual to manipulate the law.

The Law's Silence and the Invisibility of Homosexuality

To some extent, the law's denial of the rights of LGBTQ people and its silence about homosexuality in China present both challenges and opportunities. The denial of same-sex marriage has undoubtedly posed difficulties for nonheterosexual individuals, and I do not wish to minimize the struggle and pain of queer women who enter xinghun to be accepted in their families and their communities or the impact of xinghun on their same-sex partners. However, at the same time, the absence of a law that prohibits xinghun and homosexuality in general has allowed some queer individuals to use the law creatively to maintain family harmony.

The Chinese sociologist and sexologist Yinhe Li's recent writing reveals that what gays and lesbians in China are facing is ignorance and disdain (忽视和蔑视) in mainstream society rather than hate crimes and cruel oppression. The very fact that the law remains silent about homosexuality leaves many things undefined, creating blurred boundaries between legal and illegal behaviors.[28] For example, the law does not stipulate whether a marriage is valid when a nonheterosexual person enters a heterosexual marriage without revealing her sexuality to another party. Nor does the law openly regulate xinghun.

Donald Black's theorization of the relationship between law and relational distance is helpful in facilitating a better understanding of the law's lack of attention to the rights and even existence of LGBTQ people in a relation-based society such as

China. According to Black, relational distance predicts and explains the quantity of law: "Law is inactive among intimates, increasing as the distance between people increases but decreasing as this reaches the point at which people live in entirely separate worlds."[29] Black notes that intimacy provides immunity from the law because disputes between closely related people, such as members of the same family or community, tend to be handled with procedures not involving the government.[30]

Indeed, there is no space for the law to mandate the acceptance of homosexuality and secure the sense of belonging within Chinese families. For instance, Chou's research on gay adult children's experience of coming out suggests that they prefer to explain, negotiate, and bargain with their parents rather than go to court to settle family disputes.[31] This is further reinforced by the widespread belief that "even an honest official finds it hard to settle a family quarrel."[32] At the same time, echoing Black's argument, disputes resulting from xinghun rarely make it to court due to its private nature and the social stigma attached to both parties and their families. Thus, family disputes and violence associated with the process of coming out and xinghun have not attracted much attention from legal professionals.

Another factor that contributes to the law's inactive role is that China is an authoritarian regime that adheres to a civil law tradition, which reduces the likelihood that marginalized groups will challenge the law directly by going to court. Unlike the common law tradition, precedents are not binding in the Chinese legal system.[33] At the same time, advocating for legal and social changes in an authoritarian regime can be both difficult and risky for non-heterosexual individuals and their family members.[34] Thus, the law's silence on these issues results from much more complicated factors than the marginalized group's lack of interest in using it to resolve their disputes with close family members or seek attention from the public via nonformal tactics.[35] Relational distance is just a piece of the puzzle.

The mutually constitutive relationship between the law and people's perceptions of what the law should be, I argue, is another important piece. Chinese citizens' relation-based legal consciousness significantly shapes if not determines how much the Chinese state needs to rely on the law to regulate sexuality and intervene in private life and in what ways. After all, when nonheterosexual individuals focus almost exclusively on the expectations of parents and the broader community, there are already layers of informal social control mechanisms in place to prevent nonheterosexual individuals from being openly gay and fighting for marriage and childbearing rights.

Deng Jie, the volunteer leader of PFLAG China, said, "Although the law does not acknowledge same-sex marriage, we are in a much better position in terms of external pressures compared to many other countries. The Chinese state does not arrest LGBTQ folks, and there is rarely any violence on the street targeting LGBTQ people. We also do not have that much pressure from religious groups." Deng Jie was hopeful for the future because of the lack of attention from the mainstream. After all, according to Deng Jie, "it is up to us and our families to accept our sexuality." Indeed, the most profound struggle that Chinese queer subjects face is not in the public sociopolitical domain but in their private lives, especially within their immediate families.[36] The biggest challenge LGBTQ people are facing is the risk of losing the sense of belonging to their families rather than legal protections. Lan mama, a volunteer at PFLAG China and mother of a lesbian, said, "Unlike LGBTQ people in many other countries, I think Chinese LGBTQ folks care far too much about their parents' attitudes about their sexuality. Adult children's sense of security as a human being almost fully depends on their parents' acceptance. This is a huge problem."

Usually, nonheterosexual women's lack of interest in mobilizing and challenging the law is a direct result of their inescapable obligation to live up to what they consider to be parental expectations, which are largely shaped by the broader community's attitudes. The immediate consequences of failing to meet parental expectations discourage many from coming out to their parents and make the legalization of same-sex marriage unattractive to them. As Lurong, a staff member and leader of PFLAG China, suggested, family relations and reputation trumped all other considerations in the Chinese context.

> Chinese LGBTQ individuals often care more about whether their parents would accept their sexuality than anything else. I mean, legal recognition of same-sex marriage and rights to have children is important, but it is not as important as being accepted by their parents. . . . Chinese people care too much about family relations and face. Parents of queer individuals keep telling us their biggest concern is that they cannot face their relatives and friends because of the shame and loss of face resulting from their children's stigmatized identities.

Lurong's statement captures the importance of the broader community's expectations in shaping parental expectations and leftover women's construction of the latter. After all, being LGBTQ is highly stigmatized in Chinese society, and many parents such as Lin baba are more concerned about face and family reputation than the happiness of their children.

Manipulating the law for its imprimatur enables nonheterosexual leftover women to achieve the goal of meeting the perceived expectations of their parents. By going through the legal process of registering as a couple with a man and then getting a divorce, they are shielded from the gossip, disdain, and sense of shame resulting from their sexual identity. While parents still try their best to prevent their children from divorcing due to the cultural stigma of divorce and divorced women in China,[37] the stigma is generally more bearable than having a nonheterosexual child. A xinghun shifts people's attention away from queer individuals' sexuality and enables them to fit in with the majority in a relation-based society where people care a great deal about what others think of them.

When coming out to one's parents is not an option for queer leftover women, they turn to the law for protection in an unexpected way that in fact undermines the Chinese state's goal of promoting marriage and childbearing for social stability. To be specific, they rely on the law's imprimatur to gain parental and social recognition and enhance the creditability of their marriage. With the help of the law, nonheterosexual women manage to retain a sense of belonging within their families, protect their parents from gossip and condemnation, secure the right to have children legally and in an affordable manner, and gain some freedom to be themselves in private spaces. Their creative and pragmatic use of the law not only reflects the supreme role of family relationships and the significant influences of the broader community's expectations on one's choices in marriage and childbearing through the individual's family; it also reveals the lack of respect for the law among marginalized populations and people's readiness to take advantage of the law.

The Lack of Exit and Voice Options

Albert Hirschman's classic distinction between exit, voice, and loyalty is useful for making sense of categorizing xinghun as a form of legal manipulation instead of legal compliance. Focusing on people's responses to organizational decline, Hirschman points out that some members of an organization take the exit option and leave the organization, while some go for the voice option and express their dissatisfaction in order to change practices and policies.[38] The exit option is a nonconfrontational, indirect, and secret vote; the voice option instead involves the articulation of one's critical opinions directly.[39] Hirschman notes that the presence of the exit option strongly discouraged people from taking the voice option, which was more costly.[40]

There are two layers of the exit option when a nonheterosexual leftover woman considers alternative family structures: (1) leaving mainland China for a so-called queer-friendly country; and (2) cutting ties with her family. Both of these are difficult to achieve. Studies on Chinese nonheterosexual women's marital choices reveal that many financially privileged lesbian women from big cities desire to go overseas to avoid the trouble of entering xinghun, but this exit option is not available to less privileged women, such as those from relatively smaller cities because of visa requirements and lack of language skills, among other things.[41]

To some extent, going overseas enables the queer woman to avoid bringing trouble to her parents. Several queer leftover women I interviewed emphasized that they would not consider a same-sex marriage in China because society was not ready to accept this idea. Hongping, the twenty-six-year-old bisexual woman, was straightforward about her choice: "If I were living overseas somewhere more open-minded, I wouldn't mind being in a same-sex relationship openly. However, being in China and in my home province, I must choose a heterosexual marriage because what I care about most remains my parents. . . . I don't want to get my parents involved in gossip and bring them shame."

Minwei, a bisexual woman who recently returned to Fujian after receiving an MA degree in the United Kingdom, also explained to me how difficult a same-sex marriage could be in one's hometown. During her time in the United Kingdom, Minwei had a serious same-sex relationship and was planning for a life with her girlfriend. Unfortunately, they broke up shortly after their return to Fujian. Minwei suspected that if they had stayed abroad, they would still have been in relationship: "We broke up because our families gave us too much pressure to enter a heterosexual marriage as soon as possible, especially my ex-girlfriend's parents. She started to suffer from depression soon after we came back. . . . Once we were back, there are always so many expectations imposed on us and make us feel so stressed out. It is too depressing here because of the importance of maintaining guanxi and always living up to other people's expectations."

While moving overseas for a queer-friendly environment is an important motivation,[42] my interviewees mainly talked about going overseas as a strategy to be away from their parents, relatives, friends, and, more importantly, a relation-based society where boundaries are blurred. What they care most about is avoiding the immediate pressures resulting from everyday interactions with others and not having the problem of being judged based on the mainstream and heteronormative moral standards in Chinese society.

Nevertheless, leaving one's parents behind is always a tough decision. When Hongping was in a same-sex relationship several years ago, she had the desire to move far away from home "where nobody knows us" to be able to live with her girlfriend. An opportunity to relocate to Singapore knocked, but she gave it up. She said, "At that time, many of my close friends went back to my hometown to be close to their parents. Despite my strong desire to go overseas, I thought I should not be so selfish and just keep doing what I wanted." It is widely believed that staying close to parents to keep them company and take care of them is a gesture of being filial, especially when they are aging.

The relationship between the two layers of the exit option has always been complicated. Coming out usually means facing the risk of being disowned by one's parents and other family members. As Hirschman suggests, exit from a family tends to be unthinkable and comes with heavy penalties.[43] Thus, coming out is not an option for many nonheterosexual women in China, especially those who must rely on their families for financial support.[44] Huang argues that where the biogenetic family serves as the place to which queer women turn for protection and support, it is especially important for less privileged queer subjects such as those from rural areas.[45] In addition, as discussed in previous chapters, the sense of guilt and the social pressure to repay the sacrifice made by parents further reinforces the importance of remaining close to them.

Some high-quality women may consider going overseas a better option than xinghun. Lucetta Kam writes, "If cooperative marriage appropriates the surface order of a heterosexual marriage, then going abroad fulfills the normative desire of being a global and cosmopolitan Chinese subject in post-socialist China."[46] But leaving the country does not necessarily mean completely cutting ties with the relation-based society. Even if a queer woman manages to escape the country, she will likely remain deeply connected with her parents. Going overseas at best alleviates the immediate pressures imposed by parents and social circles, but the risk of ruining family relations and bringing shame to parents remains as long as the parents still value their network of connections in a relation-based community. In other words, taking advantage of both layers of the exit option is extremely difficult for nonheterosexual women, although it is not always impossible.

The voice option is also extremely risky in an authoritarian regime and a relation-based society. Similar to the exit option, there are two levels of voice when it comes to queer leftover women's choice in marriage and childbearing: resisting the law openly and confronting parents directly, both of which come with high costs. There is little to gain with the voice option, and it has the potential to push people into a more marginalized position.

The lack of both exit and voice options forces queer leftover women to adopt subtler ways of resistance, such as manipulating the law for its imprimatur to prevent family disputes and protect family reputation. Their decision to "follow" the law to achieve their goals of having children and establishing a public image of "normalcy" reflects their realistic understanding of the options available to them in the social, cultural, and legal environment of China.

CONCLUSION

The difficulties of communicating effectively about personal desires between the two generations and the emphasis on reticence about one's sexuality and expectations have created space for the prevalence of xinghun in mainland China. It is too risky to even initiate a conversation about sexuality within the family, let alone negotiate with parents to reach an agreement explicitly. Intergenerational dependence within Chinese families further reinforces the sense of guilt and responsibility to prioritize family interests over personal desires, pushing many queer individuals into xinghun. The stigma attached to homosexuality in Chinese society also accounts for nonheterosexual women's reluctance to confront parents with their "deviance." As some interviewees suggested, it would be immoral to force parents to help keep the secret by coming out to them, given the consequential loss of face and sense of shame that the parent of a queer individual experiences in Chinese society.

Law's power of recognition becomes a tool available to both high-quality and low-quality women to combat familial and societal pressures. This creative use of the law is both a result and a reflection of the importance of reticence and family harmony in Chinese society. The law's recognition of a marriage between a nonheterosexual woman and a man helps these women convince their parents, other people within their social and familial networks, and the broader community that they are "normal." It also grants them the right to have children without turning to cross-border reproductive care or underground reproductive services. Using the law's imprimatur to fulfill one's filial obligation is a prime example of relation-based legal consciousness: nonheterosexual leftover women's perceptions of and engagement with the law are shaped by their obligation as filial daughters in a social and cultural environment where fitting in matters a great deal. Xinghun is largely a performance for relatives, neighbors, colleagues, and friends so that they will be satisfied with the nonheterosexual individual's effort to fulfill her obligations.

When the Chinese legal system constrains childbearing within marriage and denies same-sex marriage for the purpose of promoting heterosexual marriage for social stability, nonheterosexual women's creative use of the law not only undermines the law's objective but also takes advantage of the law's power of recognition to alleviate pressures resulting from the expectations of parents and others.

Conclusion

In late 2023, I met Lifeng, a thirty-four-year-old woman from Fujian province, in a strip mall in Calgary on a bitter cold day with heavy snowfall. Lifeng arrived in Canada in 2014 for her undergraduate degree and recently became a permanent resident. Despite being asked to share her experience resolving disputes as a Chinese immigrant in Canada for my new research project, she ended up pouring out her family drama, which resembled the bitter stories I heard during my fieldwork in China. At the time of the interview, Lifeng was on medication for depression, and she believed what triggered her depression was her mother's tremendous pressure on her to get married and have children.

Motivated by her desire to have a grandchild as soon as possible, Lifeng's mother had come all the way from China several times a year in the past decade to look for a marital partner for her daughter at Calgary's Chinese churches and community events. As Lifeng has gotten older, her mother's approach has become bolder. Lifeng was once in an elevator of her condo complex with her mother when a stranger, a white man in his late twenties, walked in. Lifeng froze in disbelief when her mother, with an uncharacteristically chipper voice, asked about the young man's relationship status and if he wanted to marry Lifeng. "At that moment, I just thought, 'Oh gosh, I'll have to move away from this place ASAP.' It was so embarrassing that I couldn't even stand the possibility of running into that man again," Lifeng said, burying her face in her hands. To make the situation worse, her mother would soon retire and was planning to move to Canada permanently. I asked Lifeng why she would be willing to help her parents secure super visas and even permanent residency,[1] when it seemed that living apart or even cutting off contact with them for some time would be better for her mental health.

Lifeng looked at me in shock and said that cutting off contact with parents was never an option for Chinese families. She reminded me of the importance in Chinese cultures of "feeding the mother bird in return when grown up [反哺]."[2] Lifeng said, "It would be immoral to abandon my parents simply because they tried to manipulate me or pressure me to get married and have children. After all, their love and support for me was unconditional when I was growing up. Now they are aging, and they are becoming more and more stubborn and naive. In a sense, life is a circle, and they are becoming more 'childish.' I cannot abandon them at this stage." Under her piercing gaze, I had the feeling that Lifeng must have been questioning my moral integrity.

The teashop had to close early because of the bad weather. I watched Lifeng wave goodbye, then trudge toward her apartment, where her mother was waiting for her. Soon the heavy snowfall enveloped everything around me. In that silence I realized that after conducting research on this topic for a decade, I still did not have a solution or suggestions for leftover women like Lifeng.

People may say that leftover women should just communicate openly and honestly with their parents. However, I am not confident that expressing individual desires and negotiating in a more transparent manner between the generations would lead to more freedom for leftover women to choose alternative family structures. An open conversation may also mean more conflict and confrontations among close family members, which could put more pressure on these women who have already been marginalized in Chinese society because of their leftover status. I am also not sure whether Lifeng's mother's approach of "pushing bluntly" is more stressful for leftover women than the strategy of "displaying weakness," especially when the latter approach aims to manipulate adult children by using their sense of guilt. Family relations are complex. We all communicate with our family members in different styles that we think work best for us to maintain the relationships.

Fortunately, my years of research on leftover women's legal consciousness and Chinese intergenerational relationships at least allows me to identify some strategies adopted by parents to push their daughters into marriage, challenge some prevailing misunderstandings of why some leftover women choose to rush into marriage, uncover the motivations for their evasion and manipulation of the law, and reveal some characteristics of legal consciousness in authoritarian regimes and collective cultures. More importantly, this study's focus on the process during which leftover women construct their versions of parental expectations and develop strategies to deal with legal discrimination offers an opportunity for me to envision what a highly relational approach to legal consciousness may look like.

This book drew from and engaged with a wide range of literature, including legal consciousness scholarship, shared reality theory, multidisciplinary studies of leftover women, critical studies of gender and family relations in China, the discourse of suzhi and the underserving poor, the debates about xinghun, and other socio-legal studies of relationality. Combining all these sources, I developed the concept of relation-based legal consciousness to facilitate a better understanding of leftover women's compliance with the law, evasion of the law, and manipulation of the law. It is my hope that the analysis of the process during which leftover women make decisions regarding their family structures will have some implications for future studies of legal consciousness and its relational nature, as well as gender, sexuality, and family relations in Chinese cultures and beyond. I conclude this book by summarizing the theoretical contribution of relation-based legal consciousness to future law and society studies, as well as the implications of the pattern of parent-child interactions based on obligations and guilt.

RELATION-BASED LEGAL CONSCIOUSNESS, LEFTOVER WOMEN'S STRATEGIES, AND FUTURE DIRECTIONS

This study discusses leftover women's legal consciousness through their perceived obligations as filial daughters and responsible citizens in Chinese society. Using the concept of relation-based legal consciousness, I revealed how leftover women's construction of parental expectations based on the broader community's expectations and daily interactions with their parents and others shapes their compliance with the law, evasion of the law, and manipulation of the law. The concept of relation-based legal consciousness benefits from feminist relational theory's emphasis on making relationship central to the understanding of the self, but it goes one step further by illustrating the differences between the relational self in Anglo-American societies and the Chinese cultural context. Feminist relational theory's primary task is to challenge the prevailing Anglo-American conceptions of law and rights that rest so heavily on underlying conceptions of self and autonomy.[3] As Chinese society is relation-based, which requires individuals to understand relationships from the perspective of their own obligations,[4] this study argues that obligations, rather than autonomy and agency, must be front and center in making sense of leftover women's legal consciousness.

The strong sense of obligation to live up to parental expectations dilutes leftover women's interests in advocating for rights and fighting against legal discrimination. They have few illusions about what the law can do and what benefit they can receive from changes in the law; instead, they focus on developing strategies to deal with legal constraints according to their own circumstances. All these strategies are developed in response to leftover women's obligations as filial daughters and responsible citizens. The stories of Lufang, Yiyue, and many others show that their compliance with the law has little to do with their belief in its moral legitimacy. Rather, it is their strong sense of filial obligation that motivates many of them to rush into marriage and have children within a heterosexual marriage. The media campaign against leftover women and the social stigmas attached to alternative family structures have a powerful influence on leftover women's choices, but they would not be so influential if leftover women did not care so much about their obligation to protect their families' reputation and other interests.

Similarly, while queer leftover women's decision to opt for xinghun may appear as compliance with the law, this is not their intention. Their compliance is superficial and a form of resistance by manipulating the law for its imprimatur to achieve their goals of living up to their obligations as filial daughters and responsible citizens. This superficial compliance often ends up undermining the law's objectives.

Legal evasion is characterized by leftover women's indifferent attitudes toward China's legal discrimination against unmarried women's reproductive rights and their emphasis on suzhi. They stress the importance of accumulating suzhi in order to turn to cross-border or underground reproductive care. This is a prime example of how leftover women's perceptions of and engagement with the law are shaped by the broader community's legal consciousness: the broader community tends to agree with the denial of so-called low-quality women's right to have children outside marriage due to concerns about those women's lack of education and resources; at the same time, it considers high-quality leftover women's evasion of the law acceptable and even an indication of their capacity to resist the law's unequal treatment. Thus, instead of focusing their time and energy on fighting for legal rights, leftover women compete with one another to accumulate suzhi to separate themselves from the "underserving poor" and be qualified to evade the law. Ultimately, it is who has more resources and respect from the broader community that justifies the decision to evade the law without being subject to moral disapproval.

Unfortunately, even high-quality leftover women themselves end up having great difficulties exercising their privilege of being qualified to evade the law. In addition to respecting the broader community's collective legal consciousness regarding how an individual should respond to the law in a responsible way, leftover women must simultaneously live up to the expectations related to being filial daughters. The standards of filial duty vary from individual to individual, depending on financial status and family background, among other factors. As a result, while educated leftover women from urban areas with high incomes have more resources in terms of money and social connections to evade the law and have children outside marriage via cross-border or underground reproductive services, their concerns about the perceived collateral damage it will bring to their prominent family's reputation often hold them back. Ironically, leftover women from rural areas and poorer families sometimes end up having more freedom to delay or forgo marriage, especially when their parents are dependent on them for financial support.

The analysis of leftover women's strategies to deal with legal constraints captures some characteristics of legal consciousness in societies and groups that prioritize collectivism over individualism. The root cause of their lack of interest in advocating for legal changes and claiming rights may have less to do with the difficulties of making meaningful legal changes than the overwhelming pressures imposed by their close ones and those they interact with regularly in their everyday lives. It helps explain the low interest in legal mobilization and activism within certain groups and societies from the lens of groupness, belonging, and cultural sensitivity.

The influential role of the broader community's expectations and the prevalence of legal evasion in Chinese societies highlight the need to go beyond legal hegemony to discuss legal consciousness in the Chinese context. In a sense, people do not necessarily follow the law out of their belief in the legitimacy of the law and authorities but rather because of their desire to fit in with the rest of the community and protect family reputations. Their decisions and strategies to comply with, evade, or manipulate the law may be shaped more by their perceptions of their obligations as respectable members of the various communities they simultaneously belong to than the legitimacy of the law or potential legal consequences.

This study joins relational theory and recent relational legal consciousness studies to call for more attention to the relational nature of legal consciousness due to our social embeddedness. It is my hope that this study will serve as a springboard for new approaches to bridging the two existing categories of relational legal consciousness studies by emphasizing the role of obligations in shaping legal consciousness.

Despite its initial focus on how ordinary citizens' construction and interpretation of the law sustain social inequality and reinforce legal hegemony,[5] legal consciousness scholarship has expanded in the past decade or so to include the irrelevance of the law and even why people turn their backs on the law.[6] During the same period, more attention has been paid to the relational nature of legal consciousness.[7] While relational legal consciousness is a relatively new concept, recent studies have provided some hints of what a highly relational approach to legal consciousness would look like. Some legal consciousness studies analyze the process of the relational formation of legal consciousness, with a focus on the co-construction of legal consciousness;[8] others discuss the impact of close relationships on our legal consciousness through the exchange of love among family members, the desire for a sense of belonging, and the need to maintain close relationships.[9] It is inevitable for these two categories of relational legal consciousness to grow apart given their different focuses and definitions of relationality. Relation-based legal consciousness points to a possible way to bridge the two and bring them into conversation: attention to the co-construction of obligations in our families, groups, and the broader community has the potential to help us better understand the impact of relationship on our legal consciousness.

While the concept of relation-based legal consciousness focuses on the impact of relationships on legal consciousness, it draws on the literatures of the co-construction of legal consciousness to capture the process of how close relationships shape the ways in which leftover women relate to the law. Relation-based legal consciousness acknowledges that our close relationships play a significant role in our legal consciousness, but it does not take it for granted and assume that love and emotional intimacy are the foundation of or the prerequisite for such a role. Although several studies on the impact of relationships on legal consciousness have touched on obligations, they often discuss obligations as part of the individual's love for family members or the desire for a sense of belonging to the family.[10] Indeed, many people, including the leftover women I interviewed, use "love" to describe their desire to repay their parents for the latter's support when they are trying to explain why they have the obligation to prioritize the interests of their families and articulate their sense of guilt. This study calls for more scholarly attention to the nuanced differences between the feeling of "love" and the sense of "obligation" to understand the impact of relationships on our legal consciousness.

An individual's obligation within a family, a group, or her broader community is more tangible than love, given that there are often some collective standards when it comes to "obligations" of individuals. The lens of "obligation" situates the individual's sense of guilt not only in her family but also in the broader community, and thus it opens the space for us to examine the co-construction of legal consciousness in the process of making sense of the impact of relationships on legal consciousness. It is through the lens of obligations that we are able to understand leftover women's prioritization of family reputation and the interests of parents when their parents are aggressively pushing them into marriage or when there is little emotional intimacy involved.

PARENT-CHILD INTERACTIONS BASED ON OBLIGATIONS AND GUILT

Growing up under the one-child policy, many leftover women I interviewed have a strong sense of obligation to repay their parents' support over the years. Parents also feel obligated to help their daughters solve problems in everyday life. In a relation-based society, both generations are supposed to fulfill their obligations and prioritize the interests of the family in order to ensure its prosperity and well-being. After all, as Shuming Liang suggests, it is culturally inappropriate to insist on one's rights directly, and instead people in Chinese society should start with fulfilling their own obligations and then achieving rights through other people's fulfillment of theirs.[11] Not surprisingly, this relation-based pattern of parent-child interactions tends to lead to a sense of guilt among those who fail to fulfill their obligations: leftover women's filial obligation to get married and have children to protect the family's reputation and relieve parents' anxiety often gives rise to a sense of guilt, especially when their parents have done their best to fulfill the obligations of responsible parents.

In the past few decades, the flow of family resources from the older generation to the young is evident in buying homes and grandparenting in mainland China. Instead of asking the younger generation for old-age support, parents of leftover women are doing whatever they can to provide the best resources to ensure their daughters' success in terms of education, marriage, and financial and social status. Some parents frequent parental matchmaking events to find potential marital partners for their daughter, since they see it as a way to fulfill their obligations as responsible parents to help their daughters "solve the problem" of being left over in the marriage market. Others emphasize their desire and obligation to grandparent and their concerns about their declining health to urge their daughters to hurry up and have children as soon as possible. Both strategies indicate their willingness to fulfill their obligations as responsible parents and serve as reminders for their daughters to fulfill filial obligations. They intensify the sense of guilt among those who remain "left over." This sense of guilt, as I argued in chapter 1, jeopardizes effective communication between leftover women and their parents and further justifies parental intervention in their daughters' marriage and childbearing.

Given the societal pressure and gossip individual families face and the importance of maintaining family reputations in a relation-based society, parents are not necessarily being unreasonable when they urge their daughters to enter a heterosexual marriage and have children. In fact, there is never a clear line between parental expectations and the broader community's expectations in Chinese society, and leftover women must constantly refer to mainstream norms and others' expectations to interpret parental expectations and predict what works best for their parents. When parents push bluntly and even actively participate in arranging matchmaking events, a filial daughter is expected to feel grateful for their parents' efforts to help them "solve the problem" rather than accuse their parents of not respecting personal boundaries and intervening in their personal lives. It is equally if not more difficult for leftover women to discuss with their parents alternative family structures when the latter are less aggressive. Given the importance of reticence in personal desires and rights in Chinese families and the social stigma attached to leftover women, single mothers, and queer women, there is little room for left-over women to confirm what their parents really expect through explicit communication, let alone negotiate with them. The sense of guilt prompts filial daughters to construct their perception of parental expectations in a way that prioritizes the interests of their parents and often goes beyond what their parents explicitly request.

This study demonstrates how the downflow of family resources and the resulting sense of guilt may reduce effective communication among family members and marginalize the voices and desires of the younger generation, thereby reinforcing mainstream norms at the cost of people with stigmatized identities. Foregrounding the sense of obligation in the discussion of the downflow of resources within individual families and the sense of guilt resulting from the support by the older generation will help us understand the sources of pressure to live up to parental expectations, especially among those who are at the receiving end of support.

While it is based on stories of leftover women whose understandings of their obligations are shaped by the specific cultural and political contexts in mainland China, this pattern of parent-child interactions that emphasize obligations and guilt can be found in other cultural contexts too. It is my hope that the detailed analysis of the relation-based pattern of parent-child interactions and the potential impact on leftover women's legal consciousness will invite others to investigate further the influence of the sense of obligation and guilt in close relationships of various types across different cultural settings.

There are many issues concerning the relation-based pattern of parent-child interactions that I have not examined in this book. I have not explicitly addressed the impact of the sense of obligation and guilt on the mental and even physical well-being of leftover women, as well as its potential consequences for parents. I wish that I would have been able to capture some stories of leftover women whose parents were not as supportive or whose parents were toxic and kept asking instead of giving. Unfortunately, I did not have data to analyze the sense of obligation and guilt among leftover women whose parents ignored the cultural appropriateness and kept manipulating the younger generation to feed their egos. It is understandable that leftover women would not feel comfortable accusing their parents in this way in front of a researcher they had met for the first time.

Nor have I given adequate attention to the pain and sacrifices made by low-income parents who are struggling to make ends meet while providing the best for their children by skimping on their own food, clothing, and healthcare. Not all parents can afford to buy homes for their children, and not all of them have the privilege of enjoying retirement and prioritizing grandparenting. But even "small" sacrifices should not be taken lightly. I learned this from my own maternal grandmother, who passed away in 1987 at the age of sixty shortly after being diagnosed with liver cancer. During the darkest days in the 1960s and 1970s when food was scarce across mainland China, she always provided fresh meals for her six children and ate leftovers herself. Her husband and children expressed concerns, but she insisted that sour-smelling food and rice cakes and fruit with mold did not affect her health. My mother recalled that my grandmother always said to them, "Don't worry about me. It doesn't matter for me to eat them. They are just not as tasty, but they do not affect my body. Look, I am still fat." It does not take medical training to link her liver cancer at a relatively young age with the food she ate over the years. The sacrifices she made for her children continue to inspire me today. I cannot help but wonder whether filial daughters from poorer households are affected by a deeper sense of guilt resulting from their parents' hardship.

•   •   •

In December 2023, I had a brief reunion with my parents, for the first time in five years. My parents came from mainland China to see me when I attended a workshop in Singapore. During those three days, we spent most of the time together visiting parks, birding, enjoying local food, and making tea. The humidity in the air, the snails on the pavement after heavy rain, the Buddhist temples, and the Chinese street food in Singapore all reminded me of my hometown, a place I had not visited for a long time. I always said it was because of the COVID-19 pandemic and the political tension between China and Canada when I was asked why.

My parents seemed to understand that I was actually avoiding the trouble of dealing with gossip and inquiries. Indeed, I would not be surprised if the very first question I was asked by someone I had not seen for a long time was about my marital status, followed by their advice on how to find a husband and comments about the consequences of not having children. On our way to the airport, my mother suggested that it would be a great idea for them to travel to my conference site whenever I came back to Asia rather than have me go all the way home to see them and deal with gossipy aunties and neighbors. I nodded, knowing in the depth of my heart that my parents would struggle more than I did during and after my visits home. Like many leftover women I interviewed, I don't need those gossipy aunties' approval to continue living in whatever way I prefer, but all those questions and all that gossip directed at me will hurt my parents deeply.

FIELDWORK AND METHODS

Between July and November 2016, I went to Fujian province, China, to conduct my fieldwork, speaking to leftover women and their parents. I entered the field with many questions, excitement, hope, and some uncertainty about whether people would be willing to share their stories with me. I knew that my questions were highly sensitive, personal, and emotional, and leftover women might feel reluctant to disclose personal information to a researcher they had met for the first time. It was also my concern that parents of leftover women might refuse to speak with me, since they could easily learn from my research topic that I was supportive of leftover women's choices of alternative family structures. Likewise, I was not sure about how I would be able to find front-line officials to ask for information about how they implemented the law against single women's reproductive rights.

The level of trust, support, and generosity I received from my research participants, however, ended up going beyond my expectations. While I saw it as a burden for leftover women to take the time to participate in my study, many of them told me after the interviews and focus groups that they felt empowered and listened to. Some described the interview as meditative and beneficial for their mental well-being, while others became friends with other focus group participants to create a community to support one another. Parents of leftover women did not mind being interviewed, as many of them saw it as an opportunity to educate me and other leftover women about our filial obligations. Front-line officials in urban areas were cautious and found ways to point me to the information without being critical of China's population policy, while their rural counterparts shared frankly how it affected people in their villages.

FIELDWORK AND RESEARCH PARTICIPANTS

Fujian province, which is located on China's southeast coast, was an ideal research site, as it is known for its pervasive patriarchal norms and people's emphasis on kinship networks and family relations. Not surprisingly, many young locals stay in or return to Fujian after finishing their education to remain close to their families. Within Fujian itself, the most developed urban cities, Xiamen and Fuzhou, are top destinations for young professionals and migrant workers across the province. At the same time, many people feel obligated to go back to smaller cities and towns to be with their parents, although it often means having fewer career opportunities. As most studies on leftover women focus on the experience of those who live in Beijing and Shanghai, I tried to diversify the voices of leftover women by avoiding having those who could afford the high cost of living in China's political and financial hubs dominate the discussion of leftover women's experiences. With a combination of highly developed urban cities and mountainous towns and villages, Fujian offers diversity in the backgrounds of leftover women. While most interviews were conducted in urban areas, I also visited a town in the mountainous area and a fishing village in Quanzhou, as well as two villages in rural Xiamen that were undergoing rapid urbanization. My purpose in visiting small towns and villages was to include the voices of those who returned to their hometowns to stay close to their parents.

Before I started my fieldwork in China, I created an online recruitment posting about one month prior to my arrival and reached out to colleagues and friends across Fujian to help me circulate the "Call for Participation" to leftover women and parents. At the same time, I asked around in my networks to be introduced to local officials in charge of the implementation of the population policy. I then planned my visits to each place according to the schedule of my research participants and the matchmaking events happening in the local parks. Meanwhile, I contacted my colleagues who worked closely with Fujian-based LGBTQ community organizations to help me connect with staff and active members in these organizations to get information about their events.

Attending local events where my potential research participants gathered turned out to be fruitful in terms of both recruitment and observations. My visits to two parental matchmaking corners, one in Fuzhou and one in Xiamen, and participation in a LGBTQ film screening event and the post-event dinner party in Fuzhou offered great opportunities for me to interact and connect with people who had deep understandings and experiences of topics related to marriage, childbearing, sexuality, filial duty, parental expectations, and intergenerational relationships.

It was through my networking with people I met at the local LGBTQ events that I got to know and connect with LGBTQ community leaders of the national network. In October 2016, I made a trip to Guangzhou, a city in southern China close to Hong Kong, to interview people who were involved in PFLAG China, an organization that focuses on helping queer individuals come out to their parents by facilitating mutual understandings between the two generations. I interviewed four key staff members of the organization, all of whom worked closely with LGBTQ families.

My fieldwork in Fujian province primarily entailed interviews and focus groups. In total, I conducted in-depth, open-ended interviews with 51 Chinese women who are—or used to be—leftover women, as well as three focus groups with 6 to 8 women in each group. Among the 51 leftover women I interviewed, 13 were queer, 5 of whom identified as lesbian and 7 as bisexual; another woman did not attach a label to herself but emphasized that she could not imagine being in a relationship. While all the leftover women who participated in my study identified as "women," three of them mentioned certain circumstances in which they felt uncomfortable displaying femininity. Thus, I am aware of the limitations of using the term "women" to refer to all leftover women I interviewed. My use of "women" is for analytic purposes only: it is provisional and only used here to signify a social location rather than personal identification or gender expression. Not surprisingly, none of the focus group participants identified as queer in the group setting: queer women would not feel comfortable participating in focus group discussions with heterosexual women who may ask questions about their sexuality and choices; even if queer women decided to participate, they would feel reluctant to reveal their sexuality in the group setting. Similarly, leftover women who introduced their parents to me all identified as heterosexual.

During my fieldwork, I spoke to eight parents of leftover women in Fuzhou and Xiamen, either in a group or individually. Another parent, a mother of a lesbian woman, was interviewed via phone, as she felt more comfortable that way. In addition, I interviewed five local officials who oversaw the implementation of family planning and population policies to discuss enforcement at the local level and the impacts on unmarried women's choices in marriage and childbearing.

In general, each interview took approximately one to two hours, with most of them being close to two hours. Some extended to three hours when the interviewees were eager to share more of their opinions and stories. Focus groups usually lasted approximately three hours. I audio-recorded my interviews and focus groups and took notes in most sessions. In the interviews and focus groups, we discussed leftover women's pressure to marry and have children, their strategies to deal with the legal constraints, and their future plans. My research participants also asked about my experience as a leftover woman based overseas, including my understandings of my filial obligation to care for my parents psychologically and physically and my decisions regarding marriage and childbearing. The bulk of data collection took place between July and November 2016 and a follow-up field trip in December 2017. However, as most of my participants connected with me on WeChat, China's most popular messaging and networking app, I was able to keep in touch with them and follow up whenever necessary.

Throughout my fieldwork, I was fortunate to encounter many left-over women who were willing to open up to me right away and speak freely about sensitive issues. It happened naturally, and I did not think about what made it work until I left the field. I knew that my identity as a young unmarried woman born and raised in China, as well as my familiarity with the local cultures and dialects in Fujian, enabled me to cultivate good rapport with my research participants; and my genuine interest in their experiences and stories, as well as my awareness of the emotional and political sensitivity of the topic, also enabled me to gain their trust. Conducting interviews over dinner, tea, and desserts also helped, as it always created a relaxing environment for bonding. It was also true that I tried my best to make things easier for my participants by going to them and meeting at places of their convenience: sometimes it was chatting in a dark café in a run-down shopping mall late in the evening, and at times it was interviewing in homes in remote rural villages that could only be reached by scooter.

All the factors mentioned above mattered to some extent. But looking back, I believe that the trust had already been built before the interviews. After all, agreeing to participate in such a study to share highly personal stories requires a lot of trust. During my fieldwork, no one seemed to really care about reading the informed consent form that I asked them to read and sign prior to the interview. I almost felt that every time I walked them through the form and repeated what I considered important information, I was disrespecting their trust. It would also be naive to assume that they would believe in the protection provided by a foreign university by a piece of paper.

After going through my field notes and transcriptions numerous times, I came to realize that the key to gaining an initial high level of trust from research participants we have never met is our common connection to an individual who they trust. The seemingly irrelevant information my participants shared with me suddenly all became relevant, such as so-and-so said she enjoyed the interview and so-and-so was a good friend. Leftover women I met at networking events, those who had participated in my study, and even people who heard about my study briefly played a significant role in connecting me with potential research participants. It was the trust they placed in the one who connected us that led to their high trust in a researcher they had never met. The only thing left for me to do was to maintain the high level of trust through care and sensitivity during the interviews. Having the initial trust mattered a great deal, as it not only saved the time to overcome suspicion and the sense of disconnection but also made me feel comfortable being vulnerable in front of my research participants by speaking candidly when they asked about my own experiences.

At the outset of each interview, I often started with a brief introduction of my study and invited my research participants to ask me questions about myself and the research project. Not surprisingly, many of them asked about my research findings, and they were especially interested in other leftover women's thoughts and experiences. Some were curious about what motivated me to conduct this study. These were opportunities for me to demonstrate my interests and personal connection to this research and my commitment to protecting the privacy and identity of my research participants.

My affiliation with a foreign research institution and the very fact that I could be "westernized" to some extent after being physically away from mainland China for a few years ended up benefiting my fieldwork. When I asked my research participants to define or explain some concepts for me, they felt comfortable providing more information, knowing that I could benefit from some insights from people living in mainland China. Some relaxed when they realized that what I was interested in learning was more about their own experiences than their understandings of the phenomenon of leftover women and the law. I made sure that I told my research participants throughout the interview how much I appreciated their contributions and insights, and I did not hide my ignorance about things that I had never heard of or knew little about, such as the local practice of lianggu or how lesbians sought xinghun partners. Seeing that I was eager to learn from them and know about how they related to the law in everyday life, leftover women would often connect me with those who they thought knew better or had more experience on the specific topic.

I must acknowledge that at the time of my fieldwork, the environment for scholars with foreign affiliations to conduct research in China was not as bad as it is today. It was a time when ordinary citizens did not mind sharing their information with a researcher who was genuinely interested in their lived experiences, especially when the focus was on their personal lives that did not have much to do with criticizing the regime. After all, those complaints, concerns, and plans were things they felt comfortable sharing in their everyday conversations with people around them. At that time, PFLAG China was not afraid of letting the local authority know about their work, and in fact, they invited people from the government and police officials to come to their events as a way to prove the organization's commitment to promoting family harmony for the interest of the Chinese state. Focus group participants also felt safe discussing strategies to evade the law in a group setting because of the prevalence of the evasion of the one-child policy in everyday life.

The situation for field research has changed dramatically during the past few years, especially during and after the COVID-19 pandemic. As several China scholars based in Australia note, "The continued tightening of ideological control, coupled with the increasingly strained relationships between China and many Western countries since the onset of the pandemic, has further complicated the situation."[1] I shared the concerns about the impacts of the political environment on the future of China studies with many of my colleagues in terms of access to the field, safety of researchers and participants, and the resulting shift from qualitative methods to quantitative research.[2] For internationally based China scholars, especially those in countries that are part of the Five Eyes, we are also dealing with the constraints and scrutinization imposed by our host country on our research agenda related to China.[3] In the past couple of years, I have been shifting away from conducting qualitative research in mainland China due to the factors mentioned above. If this research ends up being the last project of mine based on qualitative studies in mainland China, I hope it has conveyed my deepest gratitude to all my research participants and the people who inspired me to do this work.

NOTES

1. Anning Hu and Felicia F. Tian, "Still under the Ancestors' Shadow? Ancestor Worship and Family Formation in Contemporary China," *Demographic Research* 38, no. 1 (2018): 1–36, https://doi.org/10.4054/DemRes.2018.38.1.

2. See, e.g., Patricia Ewick and Susan S. Silbey, *The Common Place of Law: Stories from Everyday Life* (Chicago: University of Chicago Press, 1998), 47–48; David M. Engel and Frank W. Munger, *Rights of Inclusion: Law and Identity in the Life Stories of Americans with Disabilities* (Chicago: University of Chicago Press, 2003); Laura Beth Nielsen, "Situating Legal Consciousness: Experiences and Attitudes of Ordinary Citizens about Law and Street Harassment," *Law & Society Review* 34, no. 4 (2000): 1055–90, https://doi.org/10.2307/3115131; Lynette J. Chua, "Legal Mobilization and Authoritarianism," *Annual Review of Law and Social Science* 15, no. 1 (2019): 355–76, https://doi.org/10.1146/annurev-lawsocsci-101518-043026; Erik D. Fritsvold, "Under the Law: Legal Consciousness and Radical Environmental Activism," *Law & Social Inquiry* 34, no. 4 (2009): 799–824, https://doi.org/10.1111/j.1747-4469.2009.01168.x; Tu Phuong Nguyen, "Law and Precariousness in an Authoritarian State: The Case of Illegal House

Construction in Vietnam," *Law & Policy* 42, no. 2 (2020): 186–203, https://doi.org/10.1111/lapo.12143; Simon Halliday and Bronwen Morgan, "I Fought the Law and the Law Won? Legal Consciousness and the Critical Imagination," *Current Legal Problems* 66, no. 1 (2013): 1–32, https://doi.org/10.1093/clp/cut002; Qian Liu, "Legal Consciousness of the Leftover Woman: Law and Qing in Chinese Family Relations," *Asian Journal of Law and Society* 5, no. 1 (2018): 7–27, https://doi.org/10.1017/als.2017.28.

3. David Engel, *The Myth of the Litigious Society: Why We Don't Sue* (Chicago: University of Chicago Press, 2016); David Engel and Jaruwan Engel, *Tort, Custom, and Karma: Globalization and Legal Consciousness in Thailand* (Stanford: Stanford University Press, 2010); Marc Hertogh, *Nobody's Law: Legal Consciousness and Legal Alienation in Everyday Life* (London: Palgrave Macmillan, 2018); Mary E. Gallagher, *Authoritarian Legality in China* (Cambridge: Cambridge University Press, 2017); Mary E. Gallagher, "Mobilizing the Law in China: 'Informed Disenchantment' and the Development of Legal Consciousness," *Law & Society Review* 40, no. 4 (2006): 783–816, http://www.jstor.org/stable/4623347.

4. Lihong Shi, *Choosing Daughters: Family Change in Rural China* (Stanford: Stanford University Press, 2017), 3.

5. Susan Greenhalgh, *Just One Child: Science and Policy in Deng's China* (Berkeley: University of California Press, 2008).

6. Zhihe Wang et al., "Ending an Era of Population Control in China: Was the One-Child Policy Ever Needed?," *American Journal of Economics and Sociology* 75, no. 4 (2016): 929–79, https://doi.org/10.1111/ajes.12160, 930, 949; Yong Cai and Wang Feng, "The Social and Sociological Consequences of China's One-Child Policy," *Annual Review of Sociology* 47, no. 1 (2021): 587–606, https://doi.org/10.1146/annurev-soc-090220-032839, 591; Kay Ann Johnson, *China's Hidden Children: Abandonment, Adoption, and the Human Costs of the One-Child Policy* (Chicago: University of Chicago Press, 2016), 2.

7. Yunxiang Yan, "The Statist Model of Family Policy Making," in *Chinese Families Upside Down: Intergenerational Dynamics and*

Neo-Familism in the Early 21st Century, ed. Yunxiang Yan (Leiden: Brill, 2021), 226.

8. Yan, "The Statist Model of Family Policy Making," 226; Deborah S. Davis, "'We Do': Parental Involvement in the Marriages of Urban Sons and Daughters," in *Chinese Families Upside Down: Intergenerational Dynamics and Neo-Familism in the Early 21st Century*, ed. Yunxiang Yan, (Leiden: Brill, 2021), 31–54.

9. Yan, "The Statist Model of Family Policy Making," 225.

10. Qian Liu, "Law's Imposition of a Heteronormative Timeline in a Rapidly Ageing Authoritarian State," *Jindal Global Law Review* 13, no. 2 (2022): 231–51, https://doi.org/10.1007/s41020-022-00177-6.

11. China Government Website, "The National Health Commission Responds to Netizens' Suggestions on 'Providing Assisted Reproductive Services for Single Women over 30 Years Old," April 14, 2023, https://www.gov.cn/hudong/2023-04/14/content_5751428 .htm.

12. Yiying Fan, "Single Mothers Forced to Pay Fines for Giving Birth," *Sixth Tone*, June 14, 2016, https://www.sixthtone.com /news/946. Since the shift to the three-child policy in 2021, a few provinces are considering eliminating or have eliminated the fine for childbearing outside marriage. However, this does not equate with the recognition of unmarried women's reproductive rights. At best, this move is to protect the rights of children born to unmarried mothers rather than grant unmarried women the right to have children. In practice, the signature of the biological father is needed in order to register the child. For more information, see Yan Yu, Lin Zhao, and Yuhang Wu, "Ten Questions on Childbirth Registration and Lifting of Marriage Restrictions: What Does It Mean for Single Mothers and Out-of-Wedlock Births?," *The Paper*, February 6, 2023, https://www.thepaper.cn/newsDetail_forward_21816605.

13. This is based on my interview with an officer overseeing the implementation of the one-child policy in a residents' committee in urban Xiamen. Interview, Ailan, October 2016.

14. Wang et al., "Ending an Era of Population Control in China."

15. For more information, see, e.g., Di Wang, "Differential

Coalescing: Re-Building the Coalition for 'Single Women's' Reproductive Rights in China," *Journal of Contemporary China* 32, no. 143 (2023): 779–93, https://doi.org/10.1080/10670564.2022.2108680.

16. Wang, "Differential Coalescing," 787.

17. Hairong Yan, *New Masters, New Servants: Migration, Development, and Women Workers in China* (Durham, NC: Duke University Press, 2008), 116.

18. Susan Greenhalgh, *Cultivating Global Citizens: Population in the Rise of China* (Cambridge, MA: Harvard University Press, 2010), 17.

19. Greenhalgh, *Cultivating Global Citizens*, 20.

20. Greenhalgh, *Cultivating Global Citizens*, 58.

21. Greenhalgh, *Cultivating Global Citizens*, 59.

22. Ann Anagnost, "The Corporeal Politics of Quality (Suzhi)," *Public Culture* 16, no. 2 (2004): 190, https://doi.org/10.1215/08992363-16-2-189.

23. Yan, *New Masters, New Servants*, 116.

24. Tamara Jacka, "Cultivating Citizens: Suzhi (Quality) Discourse in the PRC," *Positions: East Asia Cultures Critique* 17, no. 3 (2009): 523, https://doi.org/10.1215/10679847-2009-013.

25. Delia Lin, *Civilising Citizens in Post-Mao China: Understanding the Rhetoric of Suzhi* (London: Routledge, 2017), 2; Anagnost, "The Corporeal Politics," 190; Yan, "The Statist Model of Family Policy Making," 116.

26. Anagnost, "The Corporeal Politics," 194.

27. Leta Hong Fincher, *Leftover Women: The Resurgence of Gender Inequality in China* (London: Zed Books, 2014).

28. Fincher, *Leftover Women*, 12.

29. Fincher, *Leftover Women*, 4.

30. Ellen R. Judd, "Family Strategies: Fluidities of Gender, Community and Mobility in Rural West China," *China Quarterly* 204 (2010): 921–38, https://doi.org/10.1017/S0305741010001025.

31. Fincher, *Leftover Women*, 8–9, 32–35.

32. Sandy To, *China's Leftover Women: Late Marriage among Professional Women and Its Consequences* (London: Routledge, 2015).

33. To, *China's Leftover Women*, 8, 35, 162.

34. Sandy To, "Understanding Sheng Nu ('Leftover Women'): The Phenomenon of Late Marriage among Chinese Professional Women," *Symbolic Interaction* 36, no. 1 (2013): 1–20, https://doi .org/10.1002/symb.46; Sandy To, "My Mother Wants Me to Jiaru-Haomen (Marry into a Rich and Powerful Family)! Exploring the Pathways to 'Altruistic Individualism' in Chinese Professional Women's Filial Strategies of Marital Choice," *SAGE Open* 5, no. 1 (2015): 1–11, https://doi.org/10.1177/2158244014567057; To, *China's Leftover Women*.

35. To, "My Mother Wants Me to Jiaru-Haomen," 18.

36. Arianne Gaetano, "'Leftover Women': Postponing Marriage and Renegotiating Womanhood in Urban China," *Journal of Research in Gender Studies* 4, no. 2 (2014): 124–49; Chihling Liu and Robert V. Kozinets, "Courtesy Stigma Management: Social Identity Work among China's 'Leftover Women,'" *Journal of Consumer Research* 49, no. 2 (2022): 312–35, https://doi.org/10.1093/jcr /ucab065; Qian Liu, "Qualified to Be Deviant: Stigma-Management Strategies among Chinese Leftover Women," *International Journal of Law in Context* 17, no. 3 (2021): 284–300, https://doi.org/10.1017 /S1744552321000392; Tianhan Gui, "'Leftover Women' or Single by Choice: Gender Role Negotiation of Single Professional Women in Contemporary China," *Journal of Family Issues* 41, no. 11 (2020): 1956–78, https://doi.org/10.1177/0192513X20943919.

37. Gaetano, "Leftover Women."

38. Yingchun Ji, "Between Tradition and Modernity: 'Leftover' Women in Shanghai," *Journal of Marriage and Family* 77, no. 5 (2015): 1057–73, https://doi.org/10.1111/jomf.12220.

39. Liu and Kozinets, "Courtesy Stigma Management"; see also Chihling Liu and Robert V. Kozinets, "How China's 'Leftover Women' Are Using Their Financial Power to Fight the Stigma of Being Single," *The Conversation*, November 12, 2021, https://theconversation .com/how-chinas-leftover-women-are-using-their-financial-power -to-fight-the-stigma-of-being-single-171698#:~:text=The%207%20 million%20single%20women,contributors%20to%20the%20coun try's%20growth.

40. Liyan Qi, "China Is Facing a Moment of Truth about Its Low Retirement Age," *Wall Street Journal*, April 11, 2023, https://www.wsj.com/articles/china-is-facing-a-moment-of-truth-about-its-low-retirement-age-5ed9b57f.

41. Andrew B. Kipnis, *The Funeral of Mr. Wang: Life, Death, and Ghosts in Urbanizing China* (Berkeley: University of California Press, 2021), 54.

42. Qing Lin and Jingyu Mao, "'A New Job after Retirement': Negotiating Grandparenting and Intergenerational Relationships in Urban China," *China Perspectives*, no. 1 (2022): 47–56, https://doi.org/10.4000/chinaperspectives.13520.

43. Liu, "Law's Imposition of a Heteronormative Timeline."

44. Lynette J. Chua and David M. Engel, "Legal Consciousness Reconsidered," *Annual Review of Law and Social Science* 15, no. 1 (2019): 335–53, https://doi.org/10.1146/annurev-lawsocsci-101518-042717; Leisy J. Abrego, "Relational Legal Consciousness of U.S. Citizenship: Privilege, Responsibility, Guilt, and Love in Latino Mixed-Status Families," *Law & Society Review* 53, no. 3 (2019): 641–70, https://doi.org/10.1111/lasr.12414; Hsiao-Tan Wang, "Being One of Us: The Role of Mutual Recognition and Emotion in Shaping Legal Consciousness in a Taiwanese Neighbourhood Dispute," *Asian Journal of Law and Society* 10, no. 1 (2023): 131–46, https://doi.org/10.1017/als.2022.6; Qian Liu, "'Wrong' Cases and 'Wrong' Plaintiffs: Intergenerational Relationships and Legal Consciousness in China," *Journal of Law and Society* 50, no. 1 (2023): 39–58, https://doi.org/10.1111/jols.12409; Qian Liu, "Relational Legal Consciousness in the One-Child Nation," *Law & Society Review* 57, no. 2 (2023): 214–33, https://doi.org/10.1111/lasr.12649; Fabio de Sa e Silva, "Relational Legal Consciousness and Anticorruption: Lava Jato, Social Media Interactions, and the Co-Production of Law's Detraction in Brazil (2017–2019)," *Law & Society Review* 56, no. 3 (2022): 344–68, https://doi.org/10.1111/lasr.12620; Spencer Headworth, "The Power of Second-Order Legal Consciousness: Authorities' Perceptions of 'Street Policy' and Welfare Fraud Enforcement," *Law & Society Review* 54, no. 2 (2020): 320–53, https://doi.org/10.1111/lasr.12470;

Marc Hertogh, "Relational Legal Consciousness in the Punitive Welfare State: How Dutch Welfare Officials Shape Clients' Perceptions of Law," *Law & Society Review* 57, no. 3 (2023): 293–316, https://doi.org/10.1111/lasr.12663.

45. Kathryne M. Young, "Everyone Knows the Game: Legal Consciousness in the Hawaiian Cockfight," *Law & Society Review* 48, no. 3 (2014): 502, https://doi-org.ezproxy.lib.ucalgary.ca/10.1111/lasr.12094.

46. Kathryne M. Young and Hannah Chimowitz, "How Parole Boards Judge Remorse: Relational Legal Consciousness and the Reproduction of Carceral Logic," *Law & Society Review* 56, no. 2 (2022): 254–56, https://doi.org/10.1111/lasr.12601, 242.

47. Janice Nadler, "Expressive Law, Social Norms, and Social Groups," *Law & Social Inquiry* 42, no. 1 (2017): 60–75, https://doi.org/10.1111/lsi.12279, 70–71.

48. Abrego, "Relational Legal Consciousness of U.S. Citizenship," 647.

49. Qian Liu, "Relational Legal Consciousness in the One-Child Nation," *Law & Society Review* 57, no. 2 (2023): 214–33, https://doi.org/10.1111/lasr.12649; Qian Liu, "Legal Collusion: Legal Consciousness under China's One-Child Policy," *Law & Social Inquiry* (2024): 1–22, https://doi.org/10.1017/lsi.2023.79; Hsiao-Tan Wang, "Justice, Emotion, and Belonging: Legal Consciousness in a Taiwanese Family Conflict," *Law & Society Review* 53, no. 3 (2019): 764–90, https://doi.org/10.1111/lasr.12422; Wang, "Being One of Us."

50. There are a few exceptions, such as Xin He's research on migrant workers in Beijing, Lillian Su's study of the selling of counterfeit commodities in Shanghai, and my previous work on legal collusion under the one-child policy in rural Fujian. Lillian Hsiao-Ling Su, "Resistance, Evasion, and Inequality: Legal Consciousness of Intellectual Property Laws in Two Chinese Markets," *Asian Journal of Law and Society* 5, no. 1 (2018): 69–89, https://doi.org/10.1017/als.2017.31; Xin Frank He, "Legal Evasion: The Strategies of Rural-Urban Migrants to Survive in Beijing," *Canadian Journal of Law and Society* 18, no. 2 (2003): 69–90; Xin Frank He, "The

Stickiness of Legal Collusion: A Difficulty of Legal Enforcement," *International Journal of the Sociology of Law* 32, no. 2 (2004): 103–17, https://doi.org/10.1016/j.ijsl.2004.03.002; Xin Frank He, "Why Do They Not Comply with the Law? Illegality and Semi-Legality among Rural-Urban Migrant Entrepreneurs in Beijing," *Law & Society Review* 39, no. 3 (2005): 527–62, https://doi.org/10.1111/j.1540-5893 .2005.00233.x; Liu, "Legal Collusion."

51. James C. Scott, *Weapons of the Weak: Everyday Forms of Peasant Resistance* (New Haven, CT: Yale University Press, 1985).

52. He, "The Stickiness of Legal Collusion," 104.

53. Susanne Choi and Ming Luo, "Performative Family: Homosexuality, Marriage and Intergenerational Dynamics in China," *British Journal of Sociology* 67, no. 2 (2016): 260–80, https://doi .org/10.1111/1468-4446.12196.

54. I borrow the concepts of exit and voice from Albert Hirschman's classic distinction between exit, voice, and loyalty. According to Hirschman, the exit option is nonconfrontational, indirect, and secret, whereas the voice option expresses dissatisfaction and articulates critical opinions directly. See Albert Hirschman, *Exit, Voice, and Loyalty: Responses to Decline in Firms, Organizations, and States* (Cambridge, MA: Harvard University Press, 1970).

1. ANXIOUS PARENTS AND FILIAL DAUGHTERS IN THE ONE-CHILD NATION

1. While there are more leftover men than leftover women in China due to son preference in Chinese society, my observation in the field confirms that most parents who were active at matchmaking corners were looking for marital partners for their daughters. This observation has also been supported by Peidong Sun and Jun Zhang's study on parental matchmaking in Shanghai. Jun Zhang and Peidong Sun, "'When Are You Going to Get Married?' Parental Matchmaking and Middle-Class Women in Contemporary China," in *Wives, Husbands, and Lovers: Marriage and Sexuality in Hong Kong, Taiwan, and Urban China*, ed. Deborah S. Davis and Sara Friedman (Stanford: Stanford University Press, 2014).

2. Interview, Shanna, August 2016, Xiamen.

3. Elisabeth Engebretsen, "Under Pressure: Lesbian-Gay Contract Marriages and Their Patriarchal Bargains," in *Transforming Patriarchy: Chinese Families in the Twenty-First Century*, ed. Goncalo Santos and Steven Harrell (Seattle: University of Washington Press, 2016), 164.

4. Ming He and Shao-jie Zhang, "Re-Conceptualizing the Chinese Concept of Face from a Face-Sensitive Perspective: A Case Study of a Modern Chinese TV Drama," *Journal of Pragmatics* 43, no. 9 (2011): 2360–72, https://doi.org/10.1016/j.pragma.2011.03.004, 2368.

5. Engebretsen, "Under Pressure," 170.

6. Haowei Wang et al., "Adult Children's Achievements and Ageing Parents' Depressive Symptoms in China," *Ageing and Society* 42, no. 4 (2022): 896–917, https://doi.org/10.1017/S0144686X20001270.

7. Hsien-Chin Hu, "The Chinese Concepts of 'Face,'" *American Anthropologist* 46, no. 1 (1944): 45–64, https://doi.org/10.1525/aa.1944.46.1.02a00040, 45; Xiaoying Qi, "Face: A Chinese Concept in a Global Sociology," *Journal of Sociology* (Melbourne) 47, no. 3 (2011): 279–95, https://doi.org/10.1177/1440783311407692; Peter J. Buckley, Jeremy Clegg, and Hui Tan, "Cultural Awareness in Knowledge Transfer to China: The Role of *Guanxi* and *Mianzi*," *Journal of World Business* 41, no. 3 (2006): 275–88, https://doi.org/10.1016/j.jwb.2006.01.008.

8. Qi, "Face," 288.

9. Fei Wu, *Suicide and Justice: A Chinese Perspective* (London: Routledge, 2010).

10. Qian Liu, "Relational Dignity, State Law, and Chinese Leftover Women's Choices in Marriage and Childbearing," *Asian Journal of Law and Society* 8, no. 1 (2021): 151–67, https://doi.org/10.1017/als.2020.43.

11. Soroush Aslani et al., "Dignity, Face, and Honor Cultures: A Study of Negotiation Strategy and Outcomes in Three Cultures," *Journal of Organizational Behavior* 37, no. 8 (2016): 1178–1201, https://doi.org/10.1002/job.2095.

12. Jun Yi, 面子与纠纷解决: 基于法社会学的分析 (Face and Dispute Resolution: An Analysis Based on Law and Sociology), 西北民族大学学报 (Xibei Minzu Daxue Xuebao) 4 (2011): 72–78, 73.

13. Xin He and Kwai Hang Ng, "'It Must Be Rock Strong!' *Guanxi's* Impact on Judicial Decision Making in China," *American Journal of Comparative Law* 65, no. 4 (2017): 841–71, https://doi.org/10.1093/ajcl/avx041; Ji Ruan, *Guanxi, Social Capital and School Choice in China: The Rise of Ritual Capital* (Cham: Springer International, 2017), 1.

14. Yanjie Bian, *Guanxi: How China Works* (London: Polity, 2019), 3.

15. Lawrence Hsin Yang and Arthur Kleinman, "'Face' and the Embodiment of Stigma in China: The Cases of Schizophrenia and AIDS," *Social Science & Medicine* (1982) 67, no. 3 (2008): 404, https://doi.org/10.1016/j.socscimed.2008.03.011.

16. Yang and Kleinman, "'Face' and the Embodiment of Stigma in China," 401.

17. Esther C. L. Goh, *China's One-Child Policy and Multiple Caregiving: Raising Little Suns in Xiamen* (London: Routledge, 2011), 71.

18. Yunxiang Yan, *Private Life under Socialism: Love, Intimacy, and Family Change in a Chinese Village, 1949–1999* (Stanford: Stanford University Press, 2003), 177–78; Vanessa L. Fong, *Only Hope: Coming of Age under China's One-Child Policy* (Stanford: Stanford University Press, 2004).

19. Fong, *Only Hope*.

20. Bingqin Li and Hyun Bang Shin, "Intergenerational Housing Support between Retired Old Parents and Their Children in Urban China," *Urban Studies* 50, no. 16 (2013): 3225–42, https://doi.org/10.1177/0042098013483602.

21. Tsz-ming Or, "Pathways to Homeownership among Young Professionals in Urban China: The Role of Family Resources," *Urban Studies* 55, no. 11 (2018): 2391–2407, https://doi.org/10.1177/0042098017714212, 2395.

22. Goh, *China's One-Child Policy*, 65–66; Feinian Chen, Guangya Liu, and Christine A. Mair, "Intergenerational Ties in Context: Grandparents Caring for Grandchildren in China," *Social Forces* 90, no. 2 (2011): 575, https://doi.org/10.1093/sf/sor012.

23. Xiaohui Zhong and Shining He, 协商式亲密关系: 独生子女父母对家庭关系和孝道的期待 (Negotiative Intimacy: Expectations of Family Relationships and Filial Piety among Only-Child Parents),

开放时代 (Open Times), no. 1 (2014): 155–75; Li and Shin, "Intergenerational Housing Support," 3231.

24. Zhong and He, "Negotiative Intimacy."

25. Harriet Evans, "The Gender of Communication: Changing Expectations of Mothers and Daughters in Urban China," *China Quarterly* 204, no. 204 (2010): 980–1000, https://doi.org/10.1017/S0305741010001050.

26. Suowei Xiao, "Intimate Power: Intergenerational Cooperation and Conflicts in Childrearing among Urban Families," in Yan, *Chinese Families Upside Down*, 148.

27. Jieyu Liu, "Filial Piety, Love or Money? Foundation of Old-Age Support in Urban China," *Journal of Aging Studies* 64 (2023): 1–12, https://doi.org/10.1016/j.jaging.2023.101104, 10.

28. Esther C. L. Goh, Bill Y. P. Tsang, and Srinivasan Chokkanathan, "Intergenerational Reciprocity Reconsidered: The Honour and Burden of Grandparenting in Urban China," *Intersections: Gender and Sexuality in Asia and the Pacific*, no. 39 (2016), http://intersections.anu.edu.au/issue39/goh.html.

29. Goh, *China's One-Child Policy*, 65–66; Chen, Liu, and Mair, "Intergenerational Ties in Context," 575; Erin Thomason, "United in Suffering: Rural Grandparents and the Intergenerational Contributions of Care," in Yan, *Chinese Families Upside Down*, 76–102; Xiaoying Qi, "Floating Grandparents: Rethinking Family Obligation and Intergenerational Support," in Yan, *Chinese Families Upside Down*, 103–22.

30. Cong Zhang et al., "The Rise of Maternal Grandmother Child Care in Urban Chinese Families," *Journal of Marriage and Family* 81, no. 5 (2019): 1174–91, https://doi.org/10.1111/jomf.12598, 1175; Lisa Eklund, "Filial Daughter? Filial Son? How China's Young Urban Elite Negotiate Intergenerational Obligations," *Nordic Journal of Feminist and Gender Research* 26, no. 4 (2018): 297, https://doi.org/10.1080/08038740.2018.1534887.

31. Yunxiang Yan, Introduction to Yan, *Chinese Families Upside Down*, 1–30.

32. The only parent who did not mention the difficulties of having mothers-in-law as the main caregiver is a mother of a lesbian.

33. Zhang and Sun, "'When Are You Going to Get Married?'"

34. Goh, *China's One-Child Policy*, 65–66.

35. Focus group, October 2016, Xiamen.

36. Jieyu Liu, "Ageing and Familial Support: A Three-Generation Portrait from Urban China," *Ageing & Society* 44, no. 5 (2022): 1–27, https://doi.org/10.1017/S0144686X22000861, 1&24.

37. Fong, *Only Hope*, 143.

38. Fong, *Only Hope*, 143–44.

39. Harriet Evans, *The Subject of Gender: Daughters and Mothers in Urban China* (Lanham, MD: Rowman & Littlefield, 2008), 190.

40. See Yan, "Introduction," 10–11.

41. Yu Xie and Haiyan Zhu, "Do Sons or Daughters Give More Money to Parents in Urban China?," *Journal of Marriage and Family* 71, no. 1 (2009): 174–86, https://doi.org/10.1111/j.1741-3737.2008.00588.x.

42. Li and Shin, "Intergenerational Housing Support."

43. Lihong Shi, "Preparing for an 'Insured' Old Age: Insurance Purchase and Self-Support in Old Age in Rural China," *Journal of Cross-Cultural Gerontology* 33, no. 2 (2018): 183–95, https://doi.org/10.1007/s10823-018-9348-6.

44. Yan, "Introduction," 5.

45. Yan, "Introduction," 10.

46. See, e.g., Gonçalo Santos, "Multiple Mothering and Labor Migration in Rural South China," in Santos and Harrell, *Transforming Patriarchy*, 91–112.

47. For more information about these parents and the organization, see, e.g., Wei Wei and Yunxiang Yan, "Rainbow Parents and the Familial Model of Tongzhi (LGBT) Activism in Contemporary China," *Chinese Sociological Review* 53, no. 5 (2021): 451–72, https://doi.org/10.1080/21620555.2021.1981129.

48. See, e.g., To, *China's Leftover Women*.

49. Deborah S. Davis, "'We Do': Parental Involvement in the Marriages of Urban Sons and Daughters," in Yan, *Chinese Families Upside Down*, 48–51.

50. Anqi Xu and Yan Xia, "The Changes in Mainland Chinese Families during the Social Transition: A Critical Analysis," *Journal*

of Comparative Family Studies 45, no. 1 (2014): 31–53, https://doi
.org/10.3138/jcfs.45.1.31, 32.

51. Xu and Xia, "Changes in Chinese Families," 48.

2. RELATION-BASED LEGAL CONSCIOUSNESS

1. Qian Liu, "Unmarried Mothers in China and Their Feminist
Resistance: Demanding Legal Rights or Social Understanding?," in
*Gender Dynamics, Feminist Activism and Social Transformation
in China*, ed. Guoguang Wu, Yuan Feng, and Helen Lansdowne
(London: Routledge, 2019), 166–84.

2. Chua and David, "Legal Consciousness Reconsidered."

3. See, e.g., Laura Beth Nielsen, "Relational Rights: A Version for
Law and Society Scholarship," *Law & Society Review* 58, no. 1 (2024):
1–25, https://doi.org/10.1017/lsr.2023.10; Young, "Everyone Knows
the Game"; Abrego, "Relational Legal Consciousness of U.S. Citizenship"; Wang, "Being One of Us"; Liu, "'Wrong' Cases and 'Wrong'
Plaintiffs"; Liu, "Relational Legal Consciousness in the One-Child
Nation."

4. Chua and Engel, "Legal Consciousness Reconsidered," 345.

5. Shuming Liang, 中国文化要义 (Essentials of Chinese Culture)
(Shanghai: Shanghai Renmin Publishing House, 2005), 82–84;
Ambrose Yeo-chi King, "Kuan-Hsi and Network Building: A Sociological Interpretation," *Daedalus* 120, no. 2 (1991): 65, https://www
.jstor.org/stable/20025374.

6. Liang, "Essentials of Chinese Culture," 82.

7. Liang, "Essentials of Chinese Culture," 83.

8. King, "Kuan-Hsi and Network Building," 65.

9. Jennifer Nedelsky, *Law's Relations: A Relational Theory of Self,
Autonomy, and Law* (Oxford: Oxford University Press, 2011); Martha
Albertson Fineman, "The Vulnerable Subject: Anchoring Equality
in the Human Condition," *Yale Journal of Law and Feminism* 20, no. 1
(2016): 1–24, http://hdl.handle.net/20.500.13051/6993; Christine Koggel, *Perspectives on Equality: Constructing a Relational Theory* (Lanham, MD: Rowman & Littlefield, 1997); Jocelyn Downie and Jennifer

J. Llewellyn, *Being Relational: Reflections on Relational Theory and Health Law* (Vancouver: UBC Press, 2012); Susan Boyd et al., *Autonomous Motherhood? A Socio-Legal Study of Choice and Constraint* (Toronto: University of Toronto Press, 2015); Robert Leckey, *Contextual Subjects: Family, State, and Relational Theory* (Toronto: University of Toronto Press, 2008).

10. Jennifer Nedelsky, "The Relational Self as the Subject of Human Rights," in *The Subject of Human Rights*, ed. Danielle Celermajer and Alexandre Lefebvre (Stanford: Stanford University Press, 2020), 40.

11. Jennifer J. Llewellyn and Jocelyn Downie, Introduction to Downie and Llewellyn, *Being Relational*, 5; emphasis in original.

12. Christine Koggel, Ami Harbin, and Jennifer Llewellyn, "Feminist Relational Theory," *Journal of Global Ethics* 18, no. 1 (2022): 4, https://doi.org/10.1080/17449626.2022.2073702.

13. Christine Koggel, "Feminist Relational Theory: The Significance of Oppression and Structures of Power: A Commentary on 'Nondomination and the Limits of Relational Autonomy' by Danielle M. Wenner," *International Journal of Feminist Approaches to Bioethics* 13, no. 2 (2020): 52, https://doi.org/10.3138/ijfab.13.2.06.

14. Nedelsky, *Law's Relations*, 4.

15. Martha Fineman, "Introduction: Understanding Vulnerability," in *Law, Vulnerability, and the Responsive State: Beyond Equality and Liberty*, ed. Martha Fineman and Laura Spitz (London: Routledge, 2024), 4.

16. Fineman, "Introduction: Understanding Vulnerability," 8–9; Fineman, "The Vulnerable Subject," 19.

17. Fineman, "The Vulnerable Subject," 21.

18. Jennifer Nedelsky, "A Relational Approach to Law and Its Core Concepts," in *The Oxford Handbook of Feminism and Law in the United States*, ed. Deborah Brake et al. (Oxford: Oxford University Press, 2021), 61.

19. Chua and Engel, "Legal Consciousness Reconsidered."

20. Chua and Engel, "Legal Consciousness Reconsidered," 345.

21. Engel, *The Myth of the Litigious Society*, 147–48.

22. Nielsen, "Relational Rights," 2.

23. Liu, "Relational Legal Consciousness"; Liu, "Legal Collusion"; Liu, "'Kill the Chicken to Scare the Monkey.'"

24. Xiaotong Fei, *From the Soil: The Foundations of Chinese Society*, trans. Gary G. Hamilton and Wang Zheng (Berkeley: University of California Press, 1992).

25. Fei, *From the Soil*, 62–63.

26. Fei, *From the Soil*, 65.

27. Fei, *From the Soil*, 62.

28. Abrego, "Relational Legal Consciousness of U.S. Citizenship."

29. Abrego, "Relational Legal Consciousness U.S. Citizenship," 665.

30. Abrego, "Relational Legal Consciousness U.S. Citizenship," 647.

31. Leisy J. Abrego, "Renewed Optimism and Spatial Mobility: Legal Consciousness of Latino Deferred Action for Childhood Arrivals Recipients and their Families in Los Angeles," *Ethnicities* 18, no. 2 (2018): 192–207, https://doi.org/10.1177/1468796817752563.

32. Hsiao-Tan Wang, "Justice, Emotion, and Belonging: Legal Consciousness in a Taiwanese Family Conflict," *Law & Society Review* 53, no. 3 (2019): 764–90, https://doi.org/10.1111/lasr.12422.

33. Liu, "Legal Collusion," 5.

34. Wang, "Justice, Emotion, and Belonging," 771.

35. Wang, "Justice, Emotion, and Belonging," 771–73.

36. Liu, "Relational Legal Consciousness"; Liu, "Legal Collusion."

37. Engel, *The Myth of the Litigious Society*; David Engel, "Ghost Claims: Lumping in the Civil Justice System," in *Research Handbook on Civil Justice*, ed. David Engel, Anne Bloom, and Richard Jolly (Northampton, MA: Edward Elgar, forthcoming).

38. Engel, *The Myth of the Litigious Society*, 157.

39. Gerald Echterhoff and E. Tory Higgins. "Shared Reality: Construct and Mechanisms," *Current Opinion in Psychology* 23 (2018): v, https://doi.org/10.1016/j.copsyc.2018.09.003; Gerald Echterhoff, E. Tory Higgins, and John M. Levine, "Shared Reality: Experiencing Commonality with Others' Inner States about the World,"

Perspectives on Psychological Science 4, no. 5 (2017): 498, https://doi
.org/10.1111/j.1745-6924.2009.01161.x.

40. Echterhoff, Higgins, and Levine, "Shared Reality," 497.

41. Echterhoff, Higgins, and Levine, "Shared Reality," 498.

42. Echterhoff and Higgins, "Shared Reality," 23.

43. Susan Andersen and Elizabeth Przybylinski, "Shared Reality in Interpersonal Relationships," *Current Opinion in Psychology* 23 (2018): 42–46, https://doi.org/10.1016/j.copsyc.2017.11.007.

44. Andersen and Przybylinski, "Shared Reality in Interpersonal Relationships."

45. Jeanie Skorinko and Stacey Sinclair, "Shared Reality through Social Tuning of Implicit Prejudice," *Current Opinion in Psychology* 23 (2018): 109, https://doi.org/10.1016/j.copsyc.2018.02.011.

46. Echterhoff and Higgins, "Shared Reality," 23.

47. Harriet Evans, "The Gender of Communication: Changing Expectations of Mothers and Daughters in Urban China," *China Quarterly* no. 204 (2010): 980–1000, https://www.jstor.org/stable/27917842.

48. Evans, "The Gender of Communication," 997.

49. Phoebe Zhang, "Chinese LGBTQ Organisations Find Creative Ways to Survive Crackdown and Closures," *South China Morning Post*, September 3, 2023, https://www.scmp.com/news/china/politics/article/3232920/chinese-lgbtq-organisations-find-crea tive-ways-survive-crackdown-and-closures?campaign=3232920&module=perpetual_scroll_0&pgtype=article.

50. George Baylons Radics, "Human Rights in Asia," in *Global Encyclopedia of Lesbian, Gay, Bisexual, Transgender, and Queer (LGBTQ) History*, ed. Howard Chiang (Gale, 2019), 787.

51. See, e.g., de Sa e Silva, "Relational Legal Consciousness and Anticorruption"; Engel, *The Myth of the Litigious Society*; Engel, "Ghost Claims."

52. Young, "Everyone Knows the Game," 502.

53. Young and Chimowitz, "How Parole Boards Judge Remorse," 254–56.

54. Headworth, "The Power of Second-Order Legal Consciousness"; Hertogh, "Relational Legal Consciousness."

55. William Haltom and Michael McCann, *Distorting the Law: Politics, Media, and the Litigation Crisis* (Chicago: University of Chicago Press, 2004).

56. Anna Kirkland, "Think of the Hippopotamus: Rights Consciousness in the Fat Acceptance Movement," *Law & Society Review* 42, no. 2 (2008): 397–432, https://doi.org/10.1111/j.1540-5893.2008.00346.x, 399.

57. Kirkland, "Think of the Hippopotamus."

58. de Sa e Silva, "Relational Legal Consciousness and Anticorruption."

59. Fincher, *Leftover Women*, 14–43.

60. Fincher, *Leftover Women*, 6.

61. Janice Nadler, "Expressive Law, Social Norms, and Social Groups," 63.

62. Echterhoff, Higgins, and Levine, "Shared Reality," 500. Echterhoff and Higgins, "Shared Reality," v.

63. E. Tory Higgins, *Shared Reality: What Makes Us Strong and Tears Us Apart* (Oxford: Oxford University Press, 2019), 274

64. Lisa Rofel, *Desiring China: Experiments in Neoliberalism, Sexuality, and Public Culture,* (Durham, NC: Duke University Press, 2007), 94–95; Lisa Rofel, "The Traffic in Money Boys," *Positions: East Asia Cultures Critique* 18, no. 2 (2010): 427, https://doi.org/10.1215/10679847-2010-009.

65. Scholars use a variety of terms to describe this shared sense of justice, including beliefs of righteousness, perceived justice from below, morality and fairness, *qing* (normal feelings or attitudes of the public) and *li* (reasonableness), and wider normative arguments. Gallagher, *Authoritarian Legality in China*; "Mobilizing the Law in China"; Mary E. Gallagher and Yujeong Yang, "Getting Schooled: Legal Mobilization as an Educative Process," *Law & Social Inquiry* 42, no. 1 (2017): 163–94, https://doi.org/10.1111/lsi.12188; Xin He and Jing Feng, "Unfamiliarity and Procedural Justice: Litigants' Attitudes toward Civil Justice in Southern China," *Law & Society Review* 55, no. 1 (2021): 104–38, https://doi.org/10.1111/lasr.12525; Xin He, Lungang Wang, and Yang Su, "Above the Roof, beneath the Law: Perceived Justice behind Disruptive Tactics of Migrant Wage

Claimants in China," *Law & Society Review* 47, no. 4 (2023): 703–38, https://www.jstor.org/stable/43670357; Qian Liu, "Legal Consciousness of the Leftover Woman: Law and Qing in Chinese Family Relations," *Asian Journal of Law and Society* 5, no. 1 (2018): 7–27, https://doi.org/10.1017/als.2017.28; Qian Liu, "With or without You: Qing, Li, Fa, and Legal Pluralism in China," *China Law and Society Review* 5, no. 2 (2020): 88–118, https://brill.com/view/journals/clsr/5/2/article-p88_88.xml?language=en.

66. For more information, see He, "Why Do They Not Comply with the Law?"; Nguyen, "Law and Precariousness"; Liu, "Legal Collusion."

67. Kipnis, *The Funeral of Mr. Wang*; Huwy-min Lucia Liu, *Governing Death, Making Persons: The New Chinese Way of Death* (Ithaca, NY: Cornell University Press, 2023).

68. For more information about the practice of lianggu, see Liu, "Legal Consciousness of the Leftover Woman." In recent years, similar practices have appeared in other parts of China as a response to the consequences of the one-child policy. In some rich villages in rural areas of Suzhou, Jiangsu province, for example, it has become common for the two families to follow the practice of "combining two families," which shares almost all the characteristics of lianggu. See Liang Guo, 保护财产还是保护家庭？—富裕农村地区的婚姻家庭新模式 (Protection over Property or Family? New Construct of Marriage and Family in Wealthy Farming Villages), June 21, 2021, https://m.thepaper.cn/baijiahao_13198767.

69. Liu, "Legal Consciousness of the Leftover Woman."

3. SUZHI AND PARENTAL EXPECTATIONS

1. I would not have asked this question if I had not confirmed with Lin baba's daughter in advance that she was heterosexual. I was mindful of the risk involved for nonheterosexual leftover women if I asked their parents this question.

2. Wang, "Differential Coalescing."

3. Greenhalgh, *Cultivating Global Citizens*, x; Rofel, *Desiring China*, 104; Anagnost, "Corporeal Politics of Quality," 190; Andrew

Kipnis, "Neoliberalism Reified: *Suzhi* Discourse and Tropes of Neoliberalism in the People's Republic of China," *Journal of the Royal Anthropological Institute* 13, no. 2 (2007): 391, https://doi.org/10.1111/j.1467-9655.2007.00432.x.

4. Feng Xu, "Governing China's Peasant Migrants: Building Xiaokang Socialism and Harmonious Society," in *China's Governmentalities: Governing Change, Changing Government*, ed. Elaine Jeffreys (London: Routledge, 2009), 38–62; David Bray, "Building 'Community': New Strategies of Governance in Urban China," in Jeffreys, *China's Governmentalities*, 88–106; Liu, "'Kill the Chicken to Scare the Monkey.'"

5. Eva Pils, "From Authoritarian Development to Totalist Urban Reordering: The Daxing Forced Evictions Case," *China Information* 34, no. 2 (2020): 270–90, https://doi.org/10.1177/0920203X20929590, 270.

6. Andrew Kipnis, "*Suzhi:* A Keyword Approach," *China Quarterly*, no. 186 (2006): 312–13, https://www.jstor.org/stable/20192614.

7. Anagnost, "Corporeal Politics of Quality," 190; Yan, *New Masters*, 129.

8. Anagnost, "Corporeal Politics of Quality," 193.

9. Xu, "Governing China's Peasant Migrants"; Bray, "Building 'Community'"; Yan, *New Masters*; Hairong Yan, "Neoliberal Governmentality and Neohumanism: Organizing Suzhi/Value Flow through Labor Recruitment Networks," *Cultural Anthropology* 18, no. 4 (2003): 493, https://doi.org/10.1525/can.2003.18.4.493.

10. "Community building," according to Bray, is a limited form of self-governance in which "the community is expected to manage its own affairs within the operational parameters established by government authorities." Bray, "Building 'Community,'" 100–102.

11. Michael B. Katz, *The Undeserving Poor: America's Enduring Confrontation with Poverty* (Oxford: Oxford University Press, 2013).

12. Katz, *The Undeserving Poor*, 3.

13. Fincher, *Leftover Women*, 30.

14. Fincher, *Leftover Women*, 30.

15. Katz, *The Undeserving Poor*, 32.

16. Katz, *The Undeserving Poor*, 11.

17. Erving Goffman, *Stigma: Notes on the Management of Spoiled Identity* (New York: Simon & Schuster, 1986), 30.

18. Yan, *Chinese Families Upside Down*, 223.

19. Fincher, *Leftover Women*, 20.

20. Ellen R. Judd, *The Chinese Women's Movement between State and Market* (Stanford: Stanford University Press, 2002), 21.

21. Judd, *The Chinese Women's Movement between State and Market*, 27.

22. Judd, *The Chinese Women's Movement between State and Market*, 24.

23. Ke Li, *Marriage Unbound: State Law, Power, and Inequality in Contemporary China* (Stanford: Stanford University Press, 2022), 62.

24. Tao-chiu Lam, "The Local State under Reform: A Study of a County in Hainan Province, China" (PhD diss., Australian National University, 2000), https://openresearch-repository.anu.edu.au/handle/1885/3/browse?type=author&sort_by=1&order=ASC&rpp=60&etal=3&value=Lam%2C+Tao-chiu&starts_with=H.

25. Anagnost, "Corporeal Politics of Quality," 193.

26. See, e.g., Fiona Kelly, "Autonomous Motherhood and the Law: Exploring the Narratives of Canada's Single Mothers by Choice," *Canadian Journal of Family Law* 28, no. 1 (2012): 63–104; Boyd et al., *Autonomous Motherhood?* One may argue that this book's focus on reproductive rights overlooks the voice of leftover women who opt for adoption. But it is worth mentioning that adoption by single women in China is also a challenging task, despite the law's permission for a single woman over the age of thirty to adopt a child as long as she is capable of supporting it. The very fact that over 140,000 Chinese children have been adopted to families in the global north through the country's international adoption program that started in 1992 may lead many people to assume that adoption is relatively easy in China. In practice, however, it is extremely difficult for Chinese citizens to find a healthy child for adoption. Kay Johnson, a professor and author of *China's Hidden Children*, once told the *Global Times*, "I know in one medium-size official orphanage in Anhui Province, for example, they may have two or three healthy children a year. And I guess people who get one of these two

or three children probably have *guanxi* (connections) and may offer a large donation." The situation is similar in other parts of China. See Dandan Ni, "Chinese Parents Compete with Foreign Applicants to Adopt Healthy Babies," *Global Times*, April 2, 2014, https://www .globaltimes.cn/content/852341.shtml; Leslie Wang, *Outsourced Children: Orphanage Care and Adoption in Globalizing China* (Stanford: Stanford University Press, 2016), 14.

27. Liu, "Relational Legal Consciousness in the One-Child Nation"; Liu, "Legal Collusion."

28. Menglu Sheng, Congzhi Zhang, and Rongde Li, "Chinese Couples Desperate for Children Turn to Illegal Surrogacy," *Caixin Global*, May 30, 2017, https://www.caixinglobal.com/2017-05-30 /chinese-couples-desperate-for-children-turn-to-illegal-surrogacy -101095787.html.

29. Luna Sun, "China Is Second Most Costly Country to Raise a Child behind South Korea, Report Warns," *South China Morning Post*, April 30, 2023, https://www.scmp.com/economy/china-economy /article/3218920/china-second-most-costly-country-raise-child -behind-south-korea-report-warns.

30. Jenny Feng, "Average Cost of Raising a Child in Urban China Hits Almost $100,000," *The China Project*, February 23, 2022, https://thechinaproject.com/2022/02/23/average-cost-of-raising-a -child-in-urban-china-hits-almost-100000/.

31. "The Question of Early Education," *China Daily E-Paper*, May 17, 2011, http://usa.chinadaily.com.cn/epaper/2011–05/27/content _12591614.htm.

32. Teresa Kuan, *Love's Uncertainty: The Politics and Ethics of Child Rearing in Contemporary China* (Berkeley: University of California Press, 2015), 209.

33. Rofel, *Desiring China*; Shuzhen Huang and Daniel C. Brouwer, "Coming out, Coming Home, Coming With: Models of Queer Sexuality in Contemporary China," *Journal of International and Intercultural Communication* 11, no. 2 (2018): 97–116, https://doi.org/10.1080 /17513057.2017.1414867.

34. Huang and Brouwer, "Coming out, Coming Home, Coming With," 102.

35. Huang and Brouwer, "Coming out, Coming Home, Coming With," 103.

36. Timothy Hildebrandt, "Same-Sex Marriage in China? The Strategic Promulgation of a Progressive Policy and Its Impact on LGBT Activism," *Review of International Studies* 37, no. 3 (2011): 1313–33, https://doi.org/10.1017/S026021051000080X.

37. Dan Chen and Yuying Tong, "Marriage for the Sake of Parents? Adult Children's Marriage Formation and Parental Psychological Distress in China," *Journal of Marriage and Family* 83, no. 4 (2021): 1194–1211, https://doi.org/10.1111/jomf.1274; Dongjie Tao et al., "Children's Marriage and Parental Subjective Well-Being: Evidence from China," *China Economic Review* 70 (2021): 101705–18, https://doi.org/10.1016/j.chieco.2021.101705; Yumiao Zhang and Wenbin Zang, "Do the Marital Statuses of Adult Offspring Affect Their Parent's Mental Health? Empirical Evidence from China," *International Journal of Environmental Research and Public Health* 19, no. 16 (2022): 10133–51, https://doi.org/10.3390/ijerph191610133.

38. See also Liu, "Relational Legal Consciousness."

39. For a discussion of some key assumptions among some liberal social scientists, see Katz, *The Undeserving Poor*, 16.

40. Sida Liu, "Cage for the Birds: On the Social Transformation of Chinese Law, 1999–2019," *China Law and Society Review* 5, no. 2 (2021): 79, https://doi.org/10.1163/25427466-00502002.

41. Liu, "Cage for the Birds," 79.

4. MANIPULATING THE LAW
FOR ITS IMPRIMATUR

1. Shuzhen Huang and Daniel C. Brouwer, "Negotiating Performances of 'Real' Marriage in Chinese Queer Xinghun," *Women's Studies in Communication* 41, no. 2 (2018): 140–58, https://doi.org/10.1080/07491409.2018.1463581; Choi and Luo, "Performative Family"; Manlin Cai, "For the Sake of Parents? Marriages of Convenience between Lesbians and Gay Men in China," *LGBTQ+ Family: An Interdisciplinary Journal* 19, no. 3 (2023): 211–27; Tingting Liu and Chris K. K. Tan, "On the Transactionalisation of Conjugal Bonds: A Feminist

Materialist Analysis of Chinese Xinghun Marriages," *Anthropological Forum* 30, no. 4 (2020): 443–63, https://doi.org/10.1080/006 64677.2020.1855108; Min Liu, "Two Gay Men Seeking Two Lesbians: An Analysis of Xinghun (Formality Marriage) Ads on China's Tianya.Cn," *Sexuality & Culture* 17, no. 3 (2013): 494–511, https://doi .org/10.1007/s12119-012-9164-z; Engebretsen, "Under Pressure."

2. Engebretsen, "Under Pressure," 163.

3. Interview, Lurong, October 2016; Interview, Lan mama, October 2016, online.

4. Choi and Luo, "Performative Family," 264.

5. Engebretsen, "Under Pressure," 178.

6. Qingfeng Wang, 家庭出柜: 影响因素及其文化阐释 ("Coming out to Family": Influencing Factors and Its Cultural Interpretation), *Guangdong Social Sciences* 3 (2014): 189–97; Qingfeng Wang, 认同而不出柜: 中国同性恋者的生存困境 (Identifying but Not Coming out: The Survival Dilemma of Homosexuals in China) (Taipei: Shibao Publishing, 2023).

7. Choi and Luo, "Performative Family," 264.

8. Shuzhen Huang, "Reclaiming Family, Reimaging Queer Relationality," *Journal of Homosexuality* 70, no. 1 (2023): 25, https://doi .org/10.1080/00918369.2022.2106466.

9. Huang, "Reclaiming Family," 22.

10. Huang, "Reclaiming Family," 23.

11. See also Toby Miles-Johnson and Yurong Wang, "'Hidden Identities': Perceptions of Sexual Identity in Beijing," *British Journal of Sociology* 69, no. 2 (2018): 323–51, https://doi.org/10.1111/1468 -4446.12279.

12. Lan mama, the rainbow parent volunteer of PFLAG China, used "coming out" to describe her own process of digesting and accepting her daughter's sexuality and eventually getting involved in the organization. A father who participated in events organized by PFLAG, according to Lan mama, also described his decision to tell his relatives and friends about his son's sexuality as "coming out" to them.

13. Rofel, *Desiring China*, 98–102.

14. Rofel, *Desiring China*, 98.

15. Wah-Shan Chou, *Tongzhi: Politics of Same-Sex Eroticism in Chinese Societies* (London: Routledge, 2000); Wah-Shan Chou, "Homosexuality and the Cultural Politics of Tongzhi in Chinese Societies," *Journal of Homosexuality* 40, no. 3–4 (2001): 27–46, https://doi.org/10.1300/J082v40n03_03.

16. Chou, "Homosexuality and the Cultural Politics," 36.

17. Huang and Brouwer, "Coming out, Coming Home, Coming With," 97.

18. Chris K. K. Tan, "Go Home, Gay Boy! Or, Why Do Singaporean Gay Men Prefer to 'Go Home' and Not 'Come Out'?," *Journal of Homosexuality* 58, no. 6–7 (2011): 865–82, https://doi.org/10.1080/00918369.2011.581930.

19. Huang and Brouwer, "Coming out, Coming Home, Coming With," 109.

20. Huang and Brouwer, "Coming out, Coming Home, Coming With," 107.

21. Huang and Brouwer, "Coming out, Coming Home, Coming With," 108–9.

22. Engebretsen, "Under Pressure," 164.

23. Choi and Luo, "Performative Family," 276.

24. Engebretsen, "Under Pressure."

25. Choi and Luo, "Performative Family," 277.

26. Tu Phuong Nguyen has briefly touched on the manipulation of the law in her discussion of the legal consciousness of ordinary citizens in Vietnam in the contexts of early retirement and illegal house construction. For example, some workers manipulate the law by turning to brokerage and corruption to fake medical assessment in the preretirement health check so that they can retire early and obtain their lifelong pensions. However, the manipulation of the law described by Nguyen differs from nonheterosexual women's manipulation of the law in that the latter does not involve anything illegal. Tu Phuong Nguyen, *Law and Precarity: Legal Consciousness and Daily Survival in Vietnam* (Cambridge: Cambridge University Press, 2023).

27. Albert O. Hirschman, *Exit, Voice, and Loyalty: Responses to Decline in Firms, Organizations, and States* (Cambridge, MA: Harvard University Press, 1970).

28. Li, Preface to Wang, *Identifying but Not Coming Out*, 7–9.

29. Donald J. Black, *The Behavior of Law* (New York: Academic Press, 1976), 41.

30. Black, *The Behavior of Law*, 42.

31. Chou, *Tongzhi*, 279–80.

32. For more information, see Liu, "'Wrong' Cases and 'Wrong' Plaintiffs."

33. Over the past decade, in the very few cases where Chinese LGBTQ people mobilized the law to fight for the recognition of same-sex marriage and unmarried women's reproductive rights, they went to court to raise attention and spark debate more than to focus narrowly on winning the case or changing the law per se. As Lynette Chua suggests, people who invoke the law in authoritarian regimes often have practical or pressing interests that lead them to use the law for media publicity, to raise awareness, or merely to apply pressure on the recalcitrant states. Chua, "Legal Mobilization and Authoritarianism," 364; Tom Phillips, "China Court Refuses to Allow Gay Marriage in Landmark Case," *The Guardian*, April 13, 2016, https://www.theguardian.com/world/2016/apr/13/china-court-refuse-gay-marriage-landmark-case; Laurie Chen, "Chinese Woman Fighting for Fertility Rights Hopes to End Single Mother Stigma," Reuters, May 11, 2023, https://www.reuters.com/world/china/chinese-woman-fighting-fertility-rights-hopes-end-single-mother-stigma-2023-05-10/#:~:text=BEIJING%2C%20May%2010%20(Reuters),over%20reproductive%20rights%20in%20China.

34. Lynette Chua, *The Politics of Love in Myanmar: LGBT Mobilization and Human Rights as a Way of Life* (Stanford: Stanford University Press, 2019); Kevin O'Brien and Yanhua Deng, "Preventing Protest One Person at a Time: Psychological Coercion and Relational Repression in China," *China Review* 17, no. 2 (2017): 179–201, https://www.jstor.org/stable/44440175.

35. See Chua, "Legal Mobilization and Authoritarianism," 363.

36. Huang and Brouwer, "Coming out, Coming Home, Coming With," 101.

37. Ethan Michelson, *Decoupling: Gender Injustice in China's Divorce Courts* (Cambridge University Press, 2022), 57; Ethan Michelson, "Decoupling: Marital Violence and the Struggle to

Divorce in China," *American Journal of Sociology* 125, no. 2 (2019): 325–81, https://doi-org.ezproxy.lib.ucalgary.ca/10.1086/705747.

38. Hirschman, *Exit, Voice, and Loyalty*, 4.

39. Hirschman, *Exit, Voice, and Loyalty*, 16, 30.

40. Hirschman, *Exit, Voice, and Loyalty*, 40–43.

41. Lucetta Y. L. Kam, "Coming out and Going Abroad: The Chuguo Mobility of Queer Women in China," *Journal of Lesbian Studies* 24, no. 2 (2020): 126–39, https://doi.org/10.1080/10894160.2019.1622932; Yingchun Ji, Yue Liu, and Shuangshuang Yang, "A Tale of Three Cities: Distinct Marriage Strategies among Chinese Lesbians," *Journal of Gender Studies* 30, no. 5 (2021): 536–48, https://doi.org/10.1080/09589236.2021.1929098.

42. Ji, Liu, and Yang, "A Tale of Three Cities"; Maurice Kwong-Lai Poon et al., "Queer-Friendly Nation? The Experience of Chinese Gay Immigrants in Canada," *China Journal of Social Work* 10, no. 1 (2017): 23–38, https://doi.org/10.1080/17525098.2017.1300354.

43. Hirschman, *Exit, Voice, and Loyalty*, 76, 96.

44. Ji, Liu, and Yang, "A Tale of Three Cities."

45. Huang, "Reclaiming Family," 25.

46. Kam, "Coming out and Going Abroad," 137.

CONCLUSION

1. A super visa allows parents to visit their children for five years at a time. It provides multiple entries for a period up to ten years. For more information, see Immigration, Refugees and Citizenship Canada, "What Is a Super Visa," April 17, 2024, https://www.canada.ca/en/immigration-refugees-citizenship/services/visit-canada/parent-grandparent-super-visa/about.html.

2. There is an old Chinese proverb that even a raven would provide food to its mother after becoming an adult to show filial piety.

3. Nedelsky, *Law's Relations*, 5.

4. Liang, *Essentials of Chinese Culture*, 82–84.

5. Ewick and Silbey, *The Common Place of Law*; Austin Sarat, " . . . 'The Law Is All Over': Power, Resistance and the Legal Consciousness of the Welfare Poor," *Yale Journal of Law & the Humanities* 2, no. 2 (1990): 343–79; Susan Silbey, "After Legal Consciousness," *Annual*

Review of Law and Social Science 1, no. 1 (2005): 323–68, https://doi
.org/10.1146/annurev.lawsocsci.1.041604.115938.

6. Engel, *Myth of the Litigious Society*; Engel and Engel, *Tort, Custom, and Karma*; Hertogh, *Nobody's Law.*

7. Some publications may not identify themselves as being about relational legal consciousness, but their contributions to our understandings of the relational nature of legal consciousness should be acknowledged. For example, Lynette Chua discusses how LGBT activists redefine and enrich the meanings of human rights by infusing the concept with local notions of social belonging and responsibility to make it relevant and appealing; and Ke Li studies how the legal professionals' case screening in rural China is affected by their connections with clients, adversaries, and the surrounding communities, or what Li refers to as "relational embeddedness." Chua, *The Politics of Love in Myanmar*; Ke Li, "Relational Embeddedness and Socially Motivated Case Screening in the Practice of Law in Rural China," *Law & Society Review* 50, no. 4 (2016): 920–52, https://doi.org/10.1111/lasr.12235.

8. Young, "Everyone Knows the Game"; de Sa e Silva, "Relational Legal Consciousness and Anticorruption"; Young and Chimowitz, "How Parole Boards Judge Remorse"; Headworth, "The Power of Second-Order Legal Consciousness"; Hertogh, "Relational Legal Consciousness in the Punitive Welfare State."

9. Abrego, "Relational Legal Consciousness of U.S. Citizenship"; Wang, "Being One of Us"; Liu, "'Wrong' Cases and 'Wrong' Plaintiffs"; Liu, "Relational Legal Consciousness in the One-Child Nation."

10. Abrego, "Relational Legal Consciousness of U.S. Citizenship"; Abrego, "Renewed Optimism and Spatial Mobility"; Wang, "Justice, Emotion, and Belonging."

11. Liang, "Essentials of Chinese Culture," 82–84.

APPENDIX: FIELDWORK AND METHODS

1. Xiao Tan et al., "Doing Fieldwork in China during and beyond the Covid-19 Pandemic: A Study," *Made in China*, no. 1 (2023): 41, https://doi.org/10.22459/mic.08.01.2023.04.

2. Lynette Ong, *Outsourcing Repression: Everyday State Power in Contemporary China* (Oxford: Oxford University Press, 2022), 181; Di Wang and Sida Liu, "Doing Ethnography on Social Media: A Methodological Guide to the Study of Online Groups in China," *Qualitative Inquiry* 27, no. 8–9 (2021): 977–87, https://doi.org/10.1177/10778004211014610; Sida Liu and Sitao Li, "How to Do Empirical Legal Studies without Numbers?," *Hong Kong Law Journal* 53, no. 3 (2023): 1260–73.

3. Maartje de Visser, Qian Liu, and Victor V. Ramraj, "Law, Politics, and the Academy in Asia: Navigating Constraints as Public Law Scholars," *Asian Journal of Law and Society*, First View (2025): 1–23, https://doi.org/10.1017/als.2024.22.

BIBLIOGRAPHY

Abrego, Leisy J. "Relational Legal Consciousness of U.S. Citizenship: Privilege, Responsibility, Guilt, and Love in Latino Mixed-Status Families." *Law & Society Review* 53, no. 3 (2019): 641–70. https://doi.org/10.1111/lasr.12414.

———. "Renewed Optimism and Spatial Mobility: Legal Consciousness of Latino Deferred Action for Childhood Arrivals Recipients and Their Families in Los Angeles." *Ethnicities* 18, no. 2 (2018): 192–207. https://doi.org/10.1177/1468796817752563.

Anagnost, Ann. "The Corporeal Politics of Quality (Suzhi)." *Public Culture* 16, no. 2 (2004): 189–208. https://doi.org/10.1215/08992363-16-2-189.

Andersen, Susan, and Elizabeth Przybylinski. "Shared Reality in Interpersonal Relationships." *Current Opinion in Psychology* 23 (2018): 42–46. https://doi.org/10.1016/j.copsyc.2017.11.007.

Aslani, Soroush, et al. "Dignity, Face, and Honor Cultures: A Study of Negotiation Strategy and Outcomes in Three Cultures." *Journal of Organizational Behavior* 37, no. 8 (2016): 1178–1201. https://doi.org/10.1002/job.2095.

Bian, Yanjie. *Guanxi: How China Works*. London: Polity, 2019.

Black, Donald J. *The Behavior of Law*. New York: Academic Press, 1976.

Boyd, Susan et al., *Autonomous Motherhood? A Socio-Legal Study of Choice and Constraint*. Toronto: University of Toronto Press, 2015.

Bray, David. "Building 'Community': New Strategies of Governance in Urban China." In *China's Governmentalities: Governing Change, Changing Government*, edited by Elaine Jeffreys. London: Routledge, 2009.

Buckley, Peter J., Jeremy Clegg, and Hui Tan. "Cultural Awareness in Knowledge Transfer to China: The Role of *Guanxi* and *Mianzi*." *Journal of World Business* 41, no. 3 (2006): 275–88. https://doi.org/10.1016/j.jwb.2006.01.008.

Cai, Manlin. "For the Sake of Parents? Marriages of Convenience between Lesbians and Gay Men in China." *LGBTQ+ Family: An Interdisciplinary Journal* 19, no. 3 (2023): 211–27. https://doi.org/10.1080/27703371.2023.2172509.

Cai, Yong, and Wang Feng. "The Social and Sociological Consequences of China's One-Child Policy." *Annual Review of Sociology* 47, no. 1 (2021): 587–606. https://doi.org/10.1146/annurev-soc-090220-032839.

Chen, Dan, and Yuying Tong. "Marriage for the Sake of Parents? Adult Children's Marriage Formation and Parental Psychological Distress in China." *Journal of Marriage and Family* 83, no. 4 (2021): 1194–1211. https://doi.org/10.1111/jomf.1274.

Chen, Feinian, Guangya Liu, and Christine A. Mair. "Intergenerational Ties in Context: Grandparents Caring for Grandchildren in China." *Social Forces* 90, no. 2 (2011): 571–94. https://doi.org/10.1093/sf/sor012.

Chen, Laurie. "Chinese Woman Fighting for Fertility Rights Hopes to End Single mother Stigma." Reuters, May 11, 2023. https://www.reuters.com/world/china/chinese-woman-fighting-fertility-rights-hopes-end-single-mother-stigma-2023-05-10/#:~:text=BEIJING%2C%20May%2010%20(Reuters),over%20reproductive%20rights%20in%20China.

China Government Website. "The National Health Commission Responds to Netizens' Suggestions on Providing Assisted Reproductive Services for Single Women over 30 Years Old." April 14, 2023. https://www.gov.cn/hudong/2023-04/14/content_5751428.htm.

Choi, Susanne, and Ming Luo. "Performative Family: Homosexuality, Marriage and Intergenerational Dynamics in China." *British Journal of Sociology* 67, no. 2 (2016): 260–80. https://doi.org/10.1111/1468-4446.12196.

Chou, Wah-Shan. "Homosexuality and the Cultural Politics of Tongzhi in Chinese Societies." *Journal of Homosexuality* 40, no. 3–4 (2001): 27–46. https://doi.org/10.1300/J082v40n03_03.

———. *Tongzhi: Politics of Same-Sex Eroticism in Chinese Societies.* London: Routledge, 2000.

Chua, Lynette J. "Legal Mobilization and Authoritarianism." *Annual Review of Law and Social Science* 15, no. 1 (2019): 355–76. https://doi .org/10.1146/annurev-lawsocsci-101518-043026.

———. *The Politics of Love in Myanmar: LGBT Mobilization and Human Rights as a Way of Life.* Stanford: Stanford University Press, 2019.

Chua, Lynette J., and David M. Engel. "Legal Consciousness Reconsidered." *Annual Review of Law and Social Science* 15, no. 1 (2019): 335–53. https://doi.org/10.1146/annurev-lawsocsci-101518-042717.

Davis, Deborah S. "'We Do': Parental Involvement in the Marriages of Urban Sons and Daughters." In *Chinese Families Upside Down: Intergenerational Dynamics and Neo-Familism in the Early 21st Century*, edited by Yunxiang Yan, 31–54. Leiden: Brill, 2021.

de Sa e Silva, Fabio. "Relational Legal Consciousness and Anticorruption: Lava Jato, Social Media Interactions, and the Co-Production of Law's Detraction in Brazil (2017–2019)." *Law & Society Review* 56, no. 3 (2022): 344–68. https://doi.org/10.1111/lasr.12620.

de Visser, Maartje, Qian Liu, and Victor V. Ramraj. "Law, Politics, and the Academy in Asia: Navigating Constraints as Public Law Scholars." *Asian Journal of Law and Society*, First View (2025): 1–23, https:// doi.org/10.1017/als.2024.22.

Downie, Jocelyn, and Jennifer J. Llewellyn. *Being Relational: Reflections on Relational Theory and Health Law.* Vancouver: UBC Press, 2012.

Echterhoff, Gerald, and E. Tory Higgins. "Shared Reality: Construct and Mechanisms." *Current Opinion in Psychology* 23 (2018): iv–vii. https:// doi.org/10.1016/j.copsyc.2018.09.003.

Echterhoff, Gerald, E. Tory Higgins, and John M. Levine. "Shared Reality: Experiencing Commonality with Others' Inner States about the World." *Perspectives on Psychological Science* 4, no. 5 (2017): 496–521. https://doi.org/10.1111/j.1745-6924.2009.01161.x.

Eklund, Lisa. "Filial Daughter? Filial Son? How China's Young Urban Elite Negotiate Intergenerational Obligations." *Nordic Journal of*

Feminist and Gender Research 26, no. 4 (2018): 295–312. https://doi.org /10.1080/08038740.2018.1534887.

Engebretsen, Elisabeth. "Under Pressure: Lesbian-Gay Contract Marriages and Their Patriarchal Bargains." In *Transforming Patriarchy: Chinese Families in the Twenty-First Century*, edited by Gonçalo Santos and Steven Harrell, 163–81. Seattle: University of Washington Press, 2016.

Engel, David. "Ghost Claims: Lumping in the Civil Justice System." In *Research Handbook on Civil Justice*, edited by David Engel, Anne Bloom, and Richard Jolly. Northampton, MA: Edward Elgar, forthcoming.

———. *The Myth of the Litigious Society: Why We Don't Sue*. Chicago: University of Chicago Press, 2016.

Engel, David, and Jaruwan Engel. *Tort, Custom, and Karma: Globalization and Legal Consciousness in Thailand*. Stanford: Stanford University Press, 2010.

Engel, David M., and Frank W. Munger. *Rights of Inclusion: Law and Identity in the Life Stories of Americans with Disabilities*. Chicago: University of Chicago Press, 2003.

Evans, Harriet. "The Gender of Communication: Changing Expectations of Mothers and Daughters in Urban China." *China Quarterly* 204, no. 204 (2010): 980–1000. https://doi.org/10.1017/S0305741010001050.

———. *The Subject of Gender: Daughters and Mothers in Urban China*. Lanham, MD: Rowman & Littlefield, 2008.

Ewick, Patricia, and Susan S. Silbey. *The Common Place of Law: Stories from Everyday Life*. Chicago: University of Chicago Press, 1998.

Fan, Yiying. "Single Mothers Forced to Pay Fines for Giving Birth." *Sixth Tone*, June 14, 2016, https://www.sixthtone.com/news/946.

Fei, Xiaotong. *From the Soil: The Foundations of Chinese Society*. Translated by Gary G. Hamilton and Wang Zheng. Berkeley: University of California Press, 1992.

Feng, Jenny. "Average Cost of Raising a Child in Urban China Hits Almost $100,000." *The China Project*, February 23, 2022. https:// thechinaproject.com/2022/02/23/average-cost-of-raising-a-child-in -urban-china-hits-almost-100000/.

Fincher, Leta Hong. *Leftover Women: The Resurgence of Gender Inequality in China*. London: Zed Books, 2014.

Fineman, Martha. "Introduction: Understanding Vulnerability." In *Law, Vulnerability, and the Responsive State: Beyond Equality and Liberty*, edited by Martha Fineman and Laura Spitz, 1–9. London: Routledge, 2024.

———. "The Vulnerable Subject: Anchoring Equality in the Human Condition." *Yale Journal of Law and Feminism* 20, no. 1 (2016): 1–24. http://hdl.handle.net/20.500.13051/6993.

Fong, Vanessa. *Only Hope: Coming of Age under China's One-Child Policy.* Stanford: Stanford University Press, 2003.

Fritsvold, Erik D. "Under the Law: Legal Consciousness and Radical Environmental Activism." *Law & Social Inquiry* 34, no. 4 (2009): 799–824. https://doi.org/10.1111/j.1747-4469.2009.01168.x.

Gaetano, Arianne. "'Leftover Women': Postponing Marriage and Renegotiating Womanhood in Urban China." *Journal of Research in Gender Studies* 4, no. 2 (2014): 124–49.

Gallagher, Mary E. *Authoritarian Legality in China.* Cambridge: Cambridge University Press, 2017.

———. "Mobilizing the Law in China: 'Informed Disenchantment' and the Development of Legal Consciousness." *Law & Society Review* 40, no. 4 (2006): 783–816. http://www.jstor.org/stable/4623347.

Gallagher, Mary E., and Yujeong Yang. "Getting Schooled: Legal Mobilization as an Educative Process." *Law & Social Inquiry* 42, no. 1 (2017): 163–94. https://doi.org/10.1111/lsi.12188.

Goffman, Erving. *Stigma: Notes on the Management of Spoiled Identity.* New York: Simon & Schuster, 1986.

Goh, Esther C. L. *China's One-Child Policy and Multiple Caregiving: Raising Little Suns in Xiamen.* London: Routledge, 2011.

Goh, Esther C. L., Bill Y. P. Tsang, and Srinivasan Chokkanathan. "Intergenerational Reciprocity Reconsidered: The Honour and Burden of Grandparenting in Urban China." *Intersections: Gender and Sexuality in Asia and the Pacific*, no. 39 (2016), http://intersections.anu.edu.au/issue39/goh.html.

Greenhalgh, Susan. *Cultivating Global Citizens: Population in the Rise of China.* Cambridge, MA: Harvard University Press, 2010.

———. *Just One Child: Science and Policy in Deng's China.* Berkeley: University of California Press, 2008.

Gui, Tianhan. "'Leftover Women' or Single by Choice: Gender Role Negotiation of Single Professional Women in Contemporary China." *Journal of Family Issues* 41, no. 11 (2020): 1956–78. https://doi.org/10.1177/0192513X20943919.

Guo, Liang. 保护财产还是保护家庭? —富裕农村地区的婚姻家庭新模式 (Protection over Property or Family? New Construct of Marriage and Family in Wealthy Farming Villages). June 21, 2021. https://m.thepaper.cn/baijiahao_13198767.

Halliday, Simon, and Bronwen Morgan. "I Fought the Law and the Law Won? Legal Consciousness and the Critical Imagination." *Current Legal Problems* 66, no. 1 (2013): 1–32. https://doi.org/10.1093/clp/cut002.

Haltom, William, and Michael McCann. *Distorting the Law: Politics, Media, and the Litigation Crisis.* Chicago: University of Chicago Press, 2004.

He, Ming, and Shao-jie Zhang. "Re-Conceptualizing the Chinese Concept of Face from a Face-Sensitive Perspective: A Case Study of a Modern Chinese TV Drama." *Journal of Pragmatics* 43, no. 9 (2011): 2360–72. https://doi.org/10.1016/j.pragma.2011.03.004.

He, Xin Frank. "Legal Evasion: The Strategies of Rural-Urban Migrants to Survive in Beijing." *Canadian Journal of Law and Society* 18, no. 2 (2003): 69–90. https://doi.org/10.1017/S0829320100007717.

———. "The Stickiness of Legal Collusion: A Difficulty of Legal Enforcement." *International Journal of the Sociology of Law* 32, no. 2 (2004): 103–17. https://doi.org/10.1016/j.ijsl.2004.03.002.

———. "Why Do They Not Comply with the Law? Illegality and Semi-Legality among Rural-Urban Migrant Entrepreneurs in Beijing." *Law & Society Review* 39, no. 3 (2005): 527–62. https://doi.org/10.1111/j.1540-5893.2005.00233.x.

He, Xin, and Jing Feng. "Unfamiliarity and Procedural Justice: Litigants' Attitudes toward Civil Justice in Southern China." *Law & Society Review* 55, no. 1 (2021): 104–38. https://doi.org/10.1111/lasr.12525.

He, Xin, and Kwai Hang Ng. "'It Must Be Rock Strong!' *Guanxi*'s Impact on Judicial Decision Making in China." *American Journal of Comparative Law* 65, no. 4 (2017): 841–71. https://doi.org/10.1093/ajcl/avx041.

He, Xin, Lungang Wang, and Yang Su. "Above the Roof, beneath the Law: Perceived Justice behind Disruptive Tactics of Migrant Wage Claimants in China." *Law & Society Review* 47, no. 4 (2013): 703–38. https://www.jstor.org/stable/43670357.

Headworth, Spencer. "The Power of Second-Order Legal Consciousness: Authorities' Perceptions of 'Street Policy' and Welfare Fraud Enforcement." *Law & Society Review* 54, no. 2 (2020): 320–53. https://doi.org/10.1111/lasr.12470.

Hertogh, Marc. *Nobody's Law: Legal Consciousness and Legal Alienation in Everyday Life.* London: Palgrave Macmillan, 2018.

———. "Relational Legal Consciousness in the Punitive Welfare State: How Dutch Welfare Officials Shape Clients' Perceptions of Law." *Law & Society Review* 57, no. 3 (2023): 293–316. https://doi.org/10.1111/lasr.12663.

Higgins, E. Tory. *Shared Reality: What Makes Us Strong and Tears Us Apart.* Oxford: Oxford University Press, 2019.

Hildebrandt, Timothy. "Same-Sex Marriage in China? The Strategic Promulgation of a Progressive Policy and Its Impact on LGBT Activism." *Review of International Studies* 37, no. 3 (2011): 1313–33. https://doi.org/10.1017/S026021051000080X.

Hirschman, Albert O. *Exit, Voice, and Loyalty: Responses to Decline in Firms, Organizations, and States.* Cambridge, MA: Harvard University Press, 1970.

Hu, Anning, and Felicia F. Tian. "Still under the Ancestors' Shadow? Ancestor Worship and Family Formation in Contemporary China." *Demographic Research* 38, no. 1 (2018): 1–36. https://doi.org/10.4054/DemRes.2018.38.1.

Hu, Hsien-Chin. "The Chinese Concepts of 'Face.'" *American Anthropologist* 46, no. 1 (1944): 45–64. https://doi.org/10.1525/aa.1944.46.1.02a00040.

Huang, Shuzhen. "Reclaiming Family, Reimaging Queer Relationality." *Journal of Homosexuality* 70, no. 1 (2023): 17–34. https://doi.org/10.1080/00918369.2022.2106466.

Huang, Shuzhen, and Daniel C. Brouwer. "Coming out, Coming Home, Coming With: Models of Queer Sexuality in Contemporary China."

Journal of International and Intercultural Communication 11, no. 2 (2018): 97–116. https://doi.org/10.1080/17513057.2017.1414867.

———. "Negotiating Performances of 'Real' Marriage in Chinese Queer Xinghun." *Women's Studies in Communication* 41, no. 2 (2018): 140–58. https://doi.org/10.1080/07491409.2018.1463581.

Jacka, Tamara. "Cultivating Citizens: Suzhi (Quality) Discourse in the PRC." *Positions: East Asia Cultures Critique* 17, no. 3 (2009): 523–35. https://doi.org/10.1215/10679847-2009-013.

Ji, Yingchun. "Between Tradition and Modernity: 'Leftover' Women in Shanghai." *Journal of Marriage and Family* 77, no. 5 (2015): 1057–73. https://doi.org/10.1111/jomf.12220.

Ji, Yingchun, Yue Liu, and Shuangshuang Yang. "A Tale of Three Cities: Distinct Marriage Strategies among Chinese Lesbians." *Journal of Gender Studies* 30, no. 5 (2021): 536–48. https://doi.org/10.1080/0958 9236.2021.1929098.

Johnson, Kay Ann. *China's Hidden Children: Abandonment, Adoption, and the Human Costs of the One-Child Policy.* Chicago: University of Chicago Press, 2016.

Judd, Ellen R. *The Chinese Women's Movement between State and Market.* Stanford: Stanford University Press, 2002.

———. "Family Strategies: Fluidities of Gender, Community and Mobility in Rural West China." *China Quarterly* 204, no. 204 (2010): 921–38. https://doi.org/10.1017/S0305741010001025.

Kam, Lucetta Y. L. "Coming out and Going Abroad: The Chuguo Mobility of Queer Women in China." *Journal of Lesbian Studies* 24, no. 2 (2020): 126–39. https://doi.org/10.1080/10894160.2019.1622932.

Katz, Michael B. *The Undeserving Poor: America's Enduring Confrontation with Poverty.* Oxford: Oxford University Press, 2013.

Kelly, Fiona. "Autonomous Motherhood and the Law: Exploring the Narratives of Canada's Single Mothers by Choice." *Canadian Journal of Family Law* 28, no. 1 (2012): 63–104.

King, Ambrose Yeo-chi. "Kuan-Hsi and Network Building: A Sociological Interpretation." *Daedalus* 120, no. 2 (1991): 63–84. https://www .jstor.org/stable/20025374.

Kipnis, Andrew. *The Funeral of Mr. Wang: Life, Death, and Ghosts in Urbanizing China.* Berkeley: University of California Press, 2021.

———. "Neoliberalism Reified: Suzhi Discourse and Tropes of Neoliberalism in the People's Republic of China." *Journal of the Royal Anthropological Institute* 13, no. 2 (2007): 383–400. https://doi.org/10.1111/j.1467-9655.2007.00432.x.

———. "*Suzhi*: A Keyword Approach." *China Quarterly*, no. 186 (2006): 295–313. https://www.jstor.org/stable/20192614.

Kirkland, Anna. "Think of the Hippopotamus: Rights Consciousness in the Fat Acceptance Movement." *Law & Society Review* 42, no. 2 (2008): 397–432. https://doi.org/10.1111/j.1540-5893.2008.00346.x.

Koggel, Christine. "Feminist Relational Theory: The Significance of Oppression and Structures of Power: A Commentary on 'Nondomination and the Limits of Relational Autonomy' by Danielle M. Wenner." *International Journal of Feminist Approaches to Bioethics* 13, no. 2 (2020): 49–55. https://doi.org/10.3138/ijfab.13.2.06.

———. *Perspectives on Equality: Constructing a Relational Theory.* Lanham, MD: Rowman & Littlefield, 1997.

Koggel, Christine, Ami Harbin, and Jennifer Llewellyn. "Feminist Relational Theory." *Journal of Global Ethics* 18, no. 1 (2022): 1–14. https://doi.org/10.1080/17449626.2022.2073702.

Kuan, Teresa. *Love's Uncertainty: The Politics and Ethics of Child Rearing in Contemporary China.* Berkeley: University of California Press, 2015.

Lam, Tao-chiu. "The Local State under Reform: A Study of a County in Hainan Province, China." PhD diss., Australian National University, 2000. https://openresearch-repository.anu.edu.au/handle/1885/3/browse?type=author&sort_by=1&order=ASC&rpp=60&etal=3&value=Lam%2C+Tao-chiu&starts_with=H.

Leckey, Robert. *Contextual Subjects: Family, State, and Relational Theory.* Toronto: University of Toronto Press, 2008.

Li, Bingqin, and Hyun Bang Shin. "Intergenerational Housing Support between Retired Old Parents and Their Children in Urban China." *Urban Studies* 50, no. 16 (2013): 3225–42. https://doi.org/10.1177/0042098013483602.

Li, Ke. *Marriage Unbound: State Law, Power, and Inequality in Contemporary China.* Stanford: Stanford University Press, 2022.

———. "Relational Embeddedness and Socially Motivated Case Screening in the Practice of Law in Rural China." *Law & Society Review* 50, no. 4 (2016): 920–52. https://doi.org/10.1111/lasr.12235.

Li, Yinhe. Preface to 王晴锋，认同而不出柜：中国同性恋者的生存困境 (Identifying but not Coming Out: The Survival Dilemma of Homosexuals in China), by Qingfeng Wang. Taipei: Shibao Publishing, 2023.

Liang, Shuming. 中国文化要义 (Essentials of Chinese Culture). Shanghai: Shanghai Renmin Publishing House, 2005.

Lin, Delia. *Civilising Citizens in Post-Mao China: Understanding the Rhetoric of Suzhi.* London: Routledge, 2017.

Lin, Qing, and Jingyu Mao. "'A New Job after Retirement': Negotiating Grandparenting and Intergenerational Relationships in Urban China." *China Perspectives*, no. 1 (2022): 47– 56. https://doi.org/10.4000/chinaperspectives.13520.

Liu, Chihling, and Robert V. Kozinets. "Courtesy Stigma Management: Social Identity Work among China's 'Leftover Women.'" *Journal of Consumer Research* 49, no. 2 (2022): 312–35. https://doi.org/10.1093/jcr/ucab065.

———. "How China's 'Leftover Women' Are Using Their Financial Power to Fight the Stigma of Being Single." *The Conversation*, November 12, 2021. https://theconversation.com/how-chinas-left over-women-are-using-their-financial-power-to-fight-the-stigma-of -being-single-171698#:~:text=The%207%20million%20single%20 women,contributors%20to%20the%20country's%20growth.

Liu, Huwy-min Lucia. *Governing Death, Making Persons: The New Chinese Way of Death.* Ithaca, NY: Cornell University Press, 2023.

Liu, Jieyu. "Ageing and Familial Support: A Three-Generation Portrait from Urban China." *Ageing & Society* (2022): 1–27. https://doi .org/10.1017/S0144686X22000861.

———. "Filial Piety, Love or Money? Foundation of Old-Age Support in Urban China." *Journal of Aging Studies* 64 (2023): 1–12. https://doi .org/10.1016/j.jaging.2023.101104.

Liu, Min. "Two Gay Men Seeking Two Lesbians: An Analysis of Xinghun (Formality Marriage) Ads on China's Tianya.cn." *Sexuality & Culture* 17, no. 3 (2013): 494–511. https://doi.org/10.1007/s12119-012-9164-z.

Liu, Qian. "'Kill the Chicken to Scare the Monkey': Heavy Penalties, Excessive COVID-19 Control Mechanisms, and Legal Consciousness in China." *Law & Policy* 45, no. 3 (2023): 292–310. https://doi.org/10.1111/lapo.12202.

———. "Law's Imposition of a Heteronormative Timeline in a Rapidly Ageing Authoritarian State." *Jindal Global Law Review* 13, no. 2 (2022): 231–51. https://doi.org/10.1007/s41020–022-00177-6.

———. "Legal Collusion: Legal Consciousness under China's One-Child Policy." *Law & Social Inquiry* (2024): 1–22. https://doi.org/10.1017/lsi.2023.79.

———. "Legal Consciousness of the Leftover Woman: Law and Qing in Chinese Family Relations." *Asian Journal of Law and Society* 5, no. 1 (2018): 7–27. https://doi.org/10.1017/als.2017.28.

———. "Qualified to Be Deviant: Stigma-Management Strategies among Chinese Leftover Women." *International Journal of Law in Context* 17, no. 3 (2021): 284–300. https://doi.org/10.1017/S1744552321000392.

———. "Relational Dignity, State Law, and Chinese Leftover Women's Choices in Marriage and Childbearing." *Asian Journal of Law and Society* 8, no. 1 (2021): 151–67. https://doi.org/10.1017/als.2020.43.

———. "Relational Legal Consciousness in the One-Child Nation." *Law & Society Review* 57, no. 2 (2023): 214–33. https://doi.org/10.1111/lasr.12649.

———. "Unmarried Mothers in China and Their Feminist Resistance: Demanding Legal Rights or Social Understanding?" In *Gender Dynamics, Feminist Activism and Social Transformation in China*, edited by Guoguang Wu, Yuan Feng, and Helen Lansdowne, 166–84. London: Routledge, 2019.

———. "With or without You: Qing, Li, Fa, and Legal Pluralism in China." *China Law and Society Review* 5, no. 2 (2020): 88–118. https://brill.com/view/journals/clsr/5/2/article-p88_88.xml?language=en.

———. "'Wrong' Cases and 'Wrong' Plaintiffs: Intergenerational Relationships and Legal Consciousness in China." *Journal of Law and Society* 50, no. 1 (2023): 39–58. https://doi.org/10.1111/jols.12409.

Liu, Sida. "Cage for the Birds: On the Social Transformation of Chinese Law, 1999–2019." *China Law and Society Review* 5, no. 2 (2021): 66–87. https://doi.org/10.1163/25427466-00502002,79.

Liu, Sida, and Sitao Li. "How to Do Empirical Legal Studies without Numbers?" *Hong Kong Law Journal* 53, no. 3 (2023): 1260–73.

Liu, Tingting, and Chris K. K. Tan. "On the Transactionalisation of Conjugal Bonds: A Feminist Materialist Analysis of Chinese Xinghun Marriages." *Anthropological Forum* 30, no. 4 (2020): 443–63. https://doi.org/10.1080/00664677.2020.1855108.

Llewellyn, Jennifer J., and Jocelyn Downie. Introduction to *Being Relational: Reflections on Relational Theory and Health Law*, edited by Jocelyn Downie and Jennifer J. Llewellyn, 1–12. Vancouver: UBC Press, 2012.

Michelson, Ethan. *Decoupling: Gender Injustice in China's Divorce Courts*. Cambridge: Cambridge University Press, 2022.

———. "Decoupling: Marital Violence and the Struggle to Divorce in China." *American Journal of Sociology* 125, no. 2 (2019): 325–81. https://doi-org.ezproxy.lib.ucalgary.ca/10.1086/705747.

Miles-Johnson, Toby, and Yurong Wang. "'Hidden Identities': Perceptions of Sexual Identity in Beijing." *British Journal of Sociology* 69, no. 2 (2018): 323–51. https://doi.org/10.1111/1468-4446.12279.

Nadler, Janice. "Expressive Law, Social Norms, and Social Groups." *Law & Social Inquiry* 42, no. 1 (2017): 60–75. https://doi.org/10.1111/lsi.12279.

Nedelsky, Jennifer. *Law's Relations: A Relational Theory of Self, Autonomy, and Law*. Oxford: Oxford University Press, 2011.

———. "A Relational Approach to Law and Its Core Concepts." In *The Oxford Handbook of Feminism and Law in the United States*, edited by Deborah Brake et al., 57–74. Oxford: Oxford University Press, 2021.

———. "The Relational Self as the Subject of Human Rights." In *The Subject of Human Rights*, edited by Danielle Celermajer and Alexandre Lefebvre, 29–47. Stanford: Stanford University Press, 2020.

Nguyen, Tu Phuong. "Law and Precariousness in an Authoritarian State: The Case of Illegal House Construction in Vietnam." *Law & Policy* 42, no. 2 (2020): 186–203. https://doi.org/10.1111/lapo.12143.

———. *Law and Precarity: Legal Consciousness and Daily Survival in Vietnam*. Cambridge: Cambridge University Press, 2023.

Ni, Dandan. "Chinese Parents Compete with Foreign Applicants to Adopt Healthy Babies." *Global Times*, April 2, 2014. https://www.globaltimes.cn/content/852341.shtml.

Nielsen, Laura Beth. "Relational Rights: A Version for Law and Society Scholarship." *Law & Society Review* 58, no. 1 (2024): 1–25. https://doi.org/10.1017/lsr.2023.10.

———. "Situating Legal Consciousness: Experiences and Attitudes of Ordinary Citizens about Law and Street Harassment." *Law & Society Review* 34, no. 4 (2000): 1055–90. https://doi.org/10.2307/3115131.

O'Brien, Kevin, and Yanhua Deng. "Preventing Protest One Person at a Time: Psychological Coercion and Relational Repression in China," *China Review* 17, no. 2 (2017): 179–201. https://www.jstor.org/stable/44440175.

Ong, Lynette. *Outsourcing Repression: Everyday State Power in Contemporary China.* Oxford: Oxford University Press, 2022.

Or, Tsz-ming. "Pathways to Homeownership among Young Professionals in Urban China: The Role of Family Resources." *Urban Studies* 55, no. 11 (2018): 2391–2407. https://doi.org/10.1177/0042098017714212.

Phillips, Tom. "China Court Refuses to Allow Gay Marriage in Landmark Case." *The Guardian*, April 13, 2016. https://www.theguardian.com/world/2016/apr/13/china-court-refuse-gay-marriage-landmark-case.

Pils, Eva. "From Authoritarian Development to Totalist Urban Reordering: The Daxing Forced Evictions Case." *China Information* 34, no. 2 (2020): 270–90. https://doi.org/10.1177/0920203X20929590.

Poon, Maurice Kwong-Lai, et al. "Queer-Friendly Nation? The Experience of Chinese Gay Immigrants in Canada." *China Journal of Social Work* 10, no. 1 (2017): 23–38. https://doi.org/10.1080/17525098.2017.1300354.

Qi, Liyan. "China Is Facing a Moment of Truth about Its Low Retirement Age." *Wall Street Journal*, April 11, 2023. https://www.wsj.com/articles/china-is-facing-a-moment-of-truth-about-its-low-retirement-age-5ed9b57f.

Qi, Xiaoying. "Face: A Chinese Concept in a Global Sociology." *Journal of Sociology* 47, no. 3 (2011): 279–95. https://doi.org/10.1177/1440783311407692.

———. "Floating Grandparents: Rethinking Family Obligation and Intergenerational Support." In *Chinese Families Upside Down: Intergenerational Dynamics and Neo-Familism in the Early 21st Century,* edited by Yunxiang Yan, 103–22. Leiden: Brill, 2021.

————. "The Question of Early Education." *China Daily E-Paper*, May 17, 2011. http://usa.chinadaily.com.cn/epaper/2011-05/27/content_1259 1614.htm.

Radics, George Baylons. "Human Rights in Asia: The History and Current State of LGBTQ Rights in South Asia, East Asia, and Southeast Asia." In *Global Encyclopedia of Lesbian, Gay, Bisexual, Transgender, and Queer (LGBTQ) History*, edited by Howard Chiang and Anjali Aronekar, 784–89. New York: Charles Scribner's Sons, 2019.

Rofel, Lisa. *Desiring China: Experiments in Neoliberalism, Sexuality, and Public Culture*. Durham, NC: Duke University Press, 2007.

————. "The Traffic in Money Boys." *Positions: East Asia Cultures Critique* 18, no. 2 (2010): 425–58. https://doi.org/10.1215/10679847-2010-009.

Ruan, Ji. *Guanxi, Social Capital and School Choice in China: The Rise of Ritual Capital*. Cham: Springer International, 2017.

Santos, Gonçalo. "Multiple Mothering and Labor Migration in Rural South China." In *Transforming Patriarchy: Chinese Families in the Twenty-First Century*, edited by Gonçalo Santos and Stevan Harrell, 91–110. Seattle: University of Washington Press, 2016.

Sarat, Austin. " . . . 'The Law Is All Over': Power, Resistance and the Legal Consciousness of the Welfare Poor." *Yale Journal of Law and the Humanities* 2, no. 2 (1990): 343–79.

Scott, James C. *Weapons of the Weak: Everyday Forms of Peasant Resistance*. New Haven, CT: Yale University Press, 1985.

Sheng, Menglu, Congzhi Zhang and Rongde Li. "Chinese Couples Desperate for Children Turn to Illegal Surrogacy." *Caixin Global*, May 30, 2017. https://www.caixinglobal.com/2017-05-30/chinese-couples-des perate-for-children-turn-to-illegal-surrogacy-101095787.html.

Shi, Lihong. *Choosing Daughters: Family Change in Rural China*. Stanford: Stanford University Press, 2017.

————. "Preparing for an 'Insured' Old Age: Insurance Purchase and Self-Support in Old Age in Rural China." *Journal of Cross-Cultural Gerontology* 33, no. 2 (2018): 183–95. https://doi.org/10.1007/s10823 -018-9348-6.

Silbey, Susan. "After Legal Consciousness." *Annual Review of Law and Social Science* 1, no. 1 (2005): 323–68. https://doi.org/10.1146/annurev .lawsocsci.1.041604.115938.

Skorinko, Jeanie, and Stacey Sinclair. "Shared Reality through Social Tuning of Implicit Prejudice." *Current Opinion in Psychology* 23 (2018): 109–12. https://doi.org/10.1016/j.copsyc.2018.02.011.

Su, Lillian Hsiao-Ling. "Resistance, Evasion, and Inequality: Legal Consciousness of Intellectual Property Laws in Two Chinese Markets." *Asian Journal of Law and Society* 5, no. 1 (2018): 69–89. https://doi .org/10.1017/als.2017.31.

Sun, Luna. "China Is Second Most Costly Country to Raise a Child Behind South Korea, Report Warns." *South China Morning Post*, April 30, 2023. https://www.scmp.com/economy/china-economy /article/3218920/china-second-most-costly-country-raise-child-behind -south-korea-report-warns.

Tan, Chris K. K. "Go Home, Gay Boy! Or, Why Do Singaporean Gay Men Prefer to 'Go Home' and Not 'Come Out'?" *Journal of Homosexuality* 58, no. 6–7 (2011): 865–82. https://doi.org/10.1080/00918369.2011 .581930.

Tan, Xiao, et al. "Doing Fieldwork in China during and beyond the Covid-19 Pandemic: A Study." *Made in China*, no. 1 (2023): 40–47. https://doi.org/10.22459/mic.08.01.2023.04.

Tao, Dongjie, et al. "Children's Marriage and Parental Subjective Well-Being: Evidence from China." *China Economic Review* 70 (2021): 101705–18. https://doi.org/10.1016/j.chieco.2021.101705.

Thireau, Isabelle, and Linshan Hua. "One Law, Two Interpretations: Mobilizing the Labor Law in Arbitration Committees and in Letters and Visits Offices." In *Engaging the Law in China: State, Society, and Possibilities for Justice*, edited by Neil Diamant, Stanley Lubman, and Kevin O'Brien, 84–107. Stanford: Stanford University Press, 2005.

Thomason, Erin. "United in Suffering: Rural Grandparents and the Intergenerational Contributions of Care." In *Chinese Families Upside Down: Intergenerational Dynamics and Neo-Familism in the Early 21st Century*, edited by Yunxiang Yan, 76–102. Leiden: Brill, 2021.

To, Sandy. *China's Leftover Women: Late Marriage among Professional Women and Its Consequences*. London: Routledge, 2015.

———. "My Mother Wants Me to Jiaru-Haomen (Marry into a Rich and Powerful Family)! Exploring the Pathways to 'Altruistic Individualism' in Chinese Professional Women's Filial Strategies of

Marital Choice." *SAGE Open* 5, no. 1 (2015): 1–11. https://doi.org /10.1177/2158244014567057.

———. "Understanding Sheng Nu ('Leftover Women'): The Phenomenon of Late Marriage among Chinese Professional Women." *Symbolic Interaction* 36, no. 1 (2013): 1–20. https://doi.org/10.1002/symb.46.

Wang, Di. "Differential Coalescing: Re-Building the Coalition for 'Single Women's' Reproductive Rights in China." *Journal of Contemporary China* 32, no. 143 (2023): 779–93. https://doi.org/10.1080/10670564.20 22.2108680.

Wang, Di, and Sida Liu. "Doing Ethnography on Social Media: A Methodological Guide to the Study of Online Groups in China." *Qualitative Inquiry* 27, no. 8–9 (2021): 977–87. https://doi.org/10.1177 /10778004211014610.

Wang, Haowei, et al. "Adult Children's Achievements and Ageing Parents' Depressive Symptoms in China." *Ageing and Society* 42, no. 4 (2022): 896–917. https://doi.org/10.1017/S0144686X20001270.

Wang, Hsiao-Tan. "Being One of Us: The Role of Mutual Recognition and Emotion in Shaping Legal Consciousness in a Taiwanese Neighbourhood Dispute." *Asian Journal of Law and Society* 10, no. 1 (2023): 131–46. https://doi.org/10.1017/als.2022.6.

———. "Justice, Emotion, and Belonging: Legal Consciousness in a Taiwanese Family Conflict." *Law & Society Review* 53, no. 3 (2019): 764–90. https://doi.org/10.1111/lasr.12422.

Wang, Leslie. *Outsourced Children: Orphanage Care and Adoption in Globalizing China*. Stanford: Stanford University Press, 2016.

Wang, Qingfeng. 家庭出柜: 影响因素及其文化阐释 (Coming out to Family: Influencing Factors and Its Cultural Interpretation). *Guangdong Social Sciences* 3 (2014): 189–97.

———. 王晴锋, 认同而不出柜: 中国同性恋者的生存困境 (Identifying but Not Coming Out: The Survival Dilemma of Homosexuals in China). Taipei: Shibao Publishing, 2023.

Wang, Zhihe, et al. "Ending an Era of Population Control in China: Was the One-Child Policy Ever Needed?" *American Journal of Economics and Sociology* 75, no. 4 (2016): 929–79. https://doi.org/10.1111 /ajes.12160.

Wei, Wei, and Yunxiang Yan. "Rainbow Parents and the Familial Model of Tongzhi (LGBT) Activism in Contemporary China." *Chinese Sociological Review* 53, no. 5 (2021): 451–72. https://doi.org/10.1080/21 620555.2021.1981129.

Wu, Fei. *Suicide and Justice: A Chinese Perspective*. London: Routledge, 2010.

Xiao, Suowei. "Intimate Power: Intergenerational Cooperation and Conflicts in Childrearing among Urban Families." In *Chinese Families Upside Down: Intergenerational Dynamics and Neo-Familism in the Early 21st Century*, edited by Yunxiang Yan, 143–75. Leiden: Brill, 2021.

Xie, Yu, and Haiyan Zhu. "Do Sons or Daughters Give More Money to Parents in Urban China?" *Journal of Marriage and Family* 71, no. 1 (2009): 174–86. https://doi.org/10.1111/j.1741-3737.2008.00588.x.

Xu, Anqi, and Yan Xia., "The Changes in Mainland Chinese Families During the Social Transition: A Critical Analysis." *Journal of Comparative Family Studies* 45, no. 1 (2014): 31–53. https://doi.org/10.3138 /jcfs.45.1.31.

Xu, Feng. "Governing China's Peasant Migrants: Building Xiaokang Socialism and Harmonious Society." In *China's Governmentalities: Governing Change, Changing Government*, edited by Elaine Jeffreys, 38–62. London: Routledge, 2009.

Yan, Hairong. "Neoliberal Governmentality and Neohumanism: Organizing Suzhi/Value Flow through Labor Recruitment Networks." *Cultural Anthropology* 18, no. 4 (2003): 493–523. https://doi.org/10 .1525/can.2003.18.4.493.

———. *New Masters, New Servants: Migration, Development, and Women Workers in China*. Durham, NC: Duke University Press, 2008.

Yan, Yunxiang, ed. *Chinese Families Upside Down: Intergenerational Dynamics and Neo-Familism in the Early 21st Century*. Leiden: Brill, 2021.

———. *Private Life under Socialism: Love, Intimacy, and Family Change in a Chinese Village, 1949–1999*. Stanford: Stanford University Press, 2003.

———. "The Statist Model of Family Policy Making." In *Chinese Families Upside Down: Intergenerational Dynamics and Neo-Familism in the Early 21st Century*, edited by Yunxiang Yan, 223–52. Leiden: Brill, 2021.

Yang, Lawrence Hsin, and Arthur Kleinman. "'Face' and the Embodiment of Stigma in China: The Cases of Schizophrenia and AIDS." *Social Science & Medicine* 67, no. 3 (2008): 398–408. https://doi.org/10.1016/j.socscimed.2008.03.011.

Yi, Jun. 面子与纠纷解决: 基于法社会学的分析 (Face and Dispute Resolution: An Analysis Based on Law and Sociology). 西北民族大学学报 (Xibei Minzu Daxue Xuebao) 4 (2011): 72–78.

Young, Kathryne M. "Everyone Knows the Game: Legal Consciousness in the Hawaiian Cockfight." *Law & Society Review* 48, no. 3 (2014): 499–530. https://doi-org.ezproxy.lib.ucalgary.ca/10.1111/lasr.12094.

Young, Kathryne M., and Hannah Chimowitz. "How Parole Boards Judge Remorse: Relational Legal Consciousness and the Reproduction of Carceral Logic." *Law & Society Review* 56, no. 2 (2022): 254–56. https://doi.org/10.1111/lasr.12601.

Yu, Yan, Lin Zhao, and Yuhang Wu. "Ten Questions on Childbirth Registration and Lifting of Marriage Restrictions: What Does It Mean for Single Mothers and Out-of-Wedlock Births?" *The Paper*, February 6, 2023. https://www.thepaper.cn/newsDetail_forward_21816605.

Zhang, Cong, et al. "The Rise of Maternal Grandmother Child Care in Urban Chinese Families." *Journal of Marriage and Family* 81, no. 5 (2019): 1174–91. https://doi.org/10.1111/jomf.12598.

Zhang, Jun, and Peidong Sun. "'When Are You Going to Get Married?' Parental Matchmaking and Middle-Class Women in Contemporary China." In *Wives, Husbands, and Lovers: Marriage and Sexuality in Hong Kong, Taiwan, and Urban China*, edited by Deborah S. Davis and Sara Friedman, 118–44. Stanford: Stanford University Press, 2014.

Zhang, Phoebe. "Chinese LGBTQ Organisations Find Creative Ways to Survive Crackdown and Closures." *South China Morning Post*, September 3, 2023. https://www.scmp.com/news/china/politics/article/3232920/chinese-lgbtq-organisations-find-creative-ways-survive-crackdown-and-closures?campaign=3232920&module=perpetual_scroll_0&pgtype=article.

Zhang, Yumiao, and Wenbin Zang. "Do the Marital Statuses of Adult Offspring Affect Their Parent's Mental Health? Empirical

Evidence from China." *International Journal of Environmental Research and Public Health* 19, no. 16 (2022): 1–18. https://doi.org/10.3390/ijerph191610133.

Zhong, Xiaohui, and Shining He. 协商式亲密关系: 独生子女父母对家庭关系和孝道的期待 (Negotiative Intimacy: Expectations of Family Relationships and Filial Piety among Only-Child Parents). 开放时代 (Open Times), no. 1 (2014): 155–75.

INDEX

Founded in 1893,
UNIVERSITY OF CALIFORNIA PRESS
publishes bold, progressive books and journals
on topics in the arts, humanities, social sciences,
and natural sciences—with a focus on social
justice issues—that inspire thought and action
among readers worldwide.

The UC PRESS FOUNDATION
raises funds to uphold the press's vital role
as an independent, nonprofit publisher, and
receives philanthropic support from a wide
range of individuals and institutions—and from
committed readers like you. To learn more, visit
ucpress.edu/supportus.